HANDBOOK
OF THE UNITED STATES
OF AMERICA

AND

GUIDE TO EMIGRATION;

GIVING THE LATEST AND MOST COMPLETE STATISTICS
OF
THE GOVERNMENT, ARMY, NAVY, DIPLOMATIC RELATIONS, FINANCE,
REVENUE, TARIFF, LAND SALES, HOMESTEAD AND NATURALIZATION
LAWS, DEBT, POPULATION OF THE UNITED STATES, AND
EACH STATE AND CONSIDERABLE CITY, AGRICULTURAL
CONDITION, AREA FOR CULTIVATION, FOREIGN COINS
AND THEIR VALUE, FOREIGN AND DOMESTIC
POSTAGES AND LABOR TABLES, EDUCATION
AND RAILWAYS, ETC., ETC.,

FURNISHING ALL THE NECESSARY INFORMATION CONCERNING THE
COUNTRY, FOR THE SETTLER, THE BUSINESS MAN, THE MERCHANT, THE
FARMER, THE IMPORTER & THE PROFESSIONAL MAN.

First published 1880.

Published in Great Britain in 2014 by Old House books & maps
c/o Osprey Publishing, PO Box 883, Oxford OX2 9PH, UK.
c/o Osprey Publishing, PO Box 3985, New York, NY 10185-3985, USA.
Website: www.oldhousebooks.co.uk

A CIP catalogue record for this book is available from the British Library.

ISBN-13: 978 1 90840 264 6

The 'Handbook of the United States of America' which provides the basis for
this book was originally published in 1880 by Gaylord Watson, New York.

Printed in China through Asia Pacific Offsett Ltd.

IMAGE ACKNOWLEDGEMENTS
Cover images, l–r: A German immigrant ship's contract and boarding card
for New York, issued in Hamburg, 1881 (Private Collection / Peter Newark
American Pictures / The Bridgeman Art Library); Immigrant family and
their belongings on a dock, c.1912 (Mary Evans Picture Library / Everett
Collection); Photograph of the Statue of Liberty, late nineteenth century
(Library of Congress)

Library of Congress, page 122; Mary Evans Picture Library, pages 12, 64, 68,
70, 98 and 154.

14 15 16 17 18   10 9 8 7 6 5 4 3 2 1

Most of the material reproduced in this book was first published in 1880, and
contains the common spelling and terms used in everyday language of that
period. Unfortunately, a tiny number of the statistics featured were partly
illegible in the original document. Where these figures have been impossible
to determine, we have marked the missing numbers with a question mark.

INTRODUCTION

By 1880, the passions of the Civil War, now fifteen years in the past, were beginning to fade. The Reconstruction of the former Confederate states was abandoned. Federal soldiers were withdrawn from the defeated South, perhaps as a sign of a return to normalcy. Politics carried on, agitated as ever. In 1880 the United States was sharply divided between two great political parties, Republican and Democrat. In the presidential election of that year the Republican nominee, James A. Garfield of Ohio, secured a paper-thin popular majority (7,018 out of some nine million votes cast) over the Democrat Winfield Scott Hancock of Pennsylvania. Eight months later Garfield was assassinated by a mentally unstable office-seeker, Charles J. Guiteau. (Garfield was the second American president to be assassinated, following Abraham Lincoln in 1865). It was not quite the peaceful, stable democracy praised by America's warmest admirers. The union was a turbulent, divided society, in which economic and political partisanship were the dominant note.

Yet the appeal of the United States remained strong. The flood of immigrants swelled, paused, and then in the 1890s resumed its dramatic growth. Immigrants may not have been able to explain the political differences between Garfield and Hancock, but they knew something about America which remains an enduring truth. In the eyes of immigrants, America was a place of opportunity and hope.

The *Handbook of the United States of America*, published in 1880, carried its true purpose in its subtitle: *Guide to Emigration ... for The Settler, The Business Man, The Merchant, The Farmer, The Importer & The Professional Man*. It was a publication designed to inform, to present 'necessary information' about the American system of government, its policies, and the kind of economic opportunities that might shape the decisions of immigrants. There have been hundreds of similar publications, with similar titles, published in English and all the major European languages. *The National Hand-Book of Facts and Figures, historical, documentary, statistical, political, from the formation of the Government to the present time, With a full chronology of the Rebellion*, a substantial publication of over 400 pages, was published in New York in 1868. The American Social Science Association published a *Handbook for Immigrants to the United States* in 1871.

The publication of such handbooks was, if not quite a big business, part of the larger structure of promotion and publicity seeking to cater to the needs of immigrants. The whole process of emigration was an international business opportunity that was fed by the European rail lines carrying immigrants to the major seaports of Liverpool and Hamburg, where passage could be booked on the great transatlantic shipping lines for American ports. On arrival in New York, the immigrant hotels, saloons and boarding houses competed for their business. The "runners" who offered their persistent services to the newly arrived were the first to help, and the first to prey upon the immigrant.

We don't know how many immigrants actually read books about America (some certainly did), but hostile or admiring books about the American people, their manners and quirks, found a broad readership across Europe. Charles Dickens' *American Notes for General Circulation*, describing a visit to the United States in 1842, was widely resented for its satirical portrayal of American manners, and disgust at the near-universal American custom of chewing tobacco and spitting. There were in truth many sources of information about American life, from family letters sent from the New World, to newspaper reports, gossip and word-of-mouth news.

Later in the nineteenth century immigrants began to write books about their experience of coming to America. Among these, one of the most charming is *From Plotzk to Boston*, which was published in Boston in 1899 (with a foreword by 'The Dickens of the Ghetto', Israel Zangwill). It was originally written in Yiddish by Mary Antin, an eleven-year-old who traveled with her family to join their father in America. Antin went on to forge a literary career singing the praises of America. Such accounts became important ways for immigrants to find their voice. In 1880, the *Handbook of the United States of America* spoke to the experience of hundreds of thousands of immigrants. If such publications did not speak *for* the immigrant, at least they addressed the world in which immigrants were making their way.

The census returns of 1850 provide the first solid figures we have about the scale of foreign-born inhabitants in the United States: 2,244,602 'foreigners', virtually all drawn from Northern Europe, had settled in the

United States. A decade later, in 1860, the immigrant population had risen to 4,138,697. Immigrant numbers grew more slowly in the 1860s, due to the Civil War and economic hard times: 5,567,229 in 1870, and a million increase to 6,679,943 in 1880.

Immigrants came from increasingly diverse places, bringing with them languages, values, and expectations which changed America – and largely for the better. There were 184,000 Germans living in Wisconsin in 1880 and 370,000 Germans in New York City, with many settling in 'Kleindeutschland' or Dutchtown, east of the Bowery. The German population in Chicago in 1900, some 470,000 strong, made up one fourth of the city's population. Nonetheless it overstates the case to claim that the United States was a 'Nation of Immigrants', the title given to a book written by Senator John F. Kennedy in 1958, and usefully employed by columnists and politicians ever after: 'We define ourselves as a nation of immigrants', remarked President Obama in an address given in Las Vegas in January 2013, shortly after he was inaugurated for his second term as president. 'The promise we see in those who come here from every corner of the globe, that's always been one of our greatest strengths.'

Not everyone has agreed with that proud assertion. There was no golden age of sympathy for foreigners in the nineteenth century. There was a long history in America of hostility to immigrants, often expressed as anti-Roman Catholicism. The experience of many immigrants was in no small measure one of struggle, disappointment, frustration, and uncertainty. Hyphenated Americans (as they were called) came under strong pressure to learn English and enter fully into American life. In a lecture in 1893, Theodore Roosevelt, then a member of the United States Civil Service Commission, claimed that 'We have a right to demand that every man, native born or foreign born, shall in American life act merely as an American... we don't wish any hyphenated Americans; we do not wish you to act as Irish-Americans, or British-Americans, or native Americans, but as Americans pure and simple.'

The call for the Americanization of the immigrants contained an 'or else', an implicit threat. But the preferred view, articulated in 'The New Colossus', an 1883 poem by Emma Lazarus, was of an outstretched hand, welcoming the 'huddled masses yearning to breathe free':

> Give me your tired, your poor,
> Your huddled masses yearning to breathe free,

The wretched refuse of your teeming shore.
Send these, the homeless, tempest-tost to me,
I lift my lamp beside the golden door.

Lazarus' poem was written in November 1883 at the request of Mrs. Burton Harrison, novelist and New York socialite, who solicited literary manuscripts for a charity auction in aid of the Bartholdi Pedestal Fund. Lazarus' poem became the interpretive gloss on 'Liberty Enlightening the World', the dramatic statue by the French sculptor Frédéric Auguste Bartholdi which occupies pride of place in New York Harbor. A bronze plaque containing the poem was placed at the base of the statue in 1903.

The American 'success' story, from Benjamin Franklin's *Poor Richard's Almanac* to Horatio Alger's tales of poor boys who made good, was central to American popular culture. Alger's *Ragged Dick* novels stood upon the shoulders of a world of pamphlets, sermons, biographies, speeches, popular novels and books for younger readers, all making clear that the American story portrayed a man who rose to success from poverty and lowly circumstances. Presidents (Andrew Jackson, Abraham Lincoln), industrialists, financiers, merchants, inventors and civic leaders were portrayed as living embodiments of that story. What Americans expected of the immigrants, their 'Americanization', came with the firm belief that the model of the 'poor boy who makes good' would serve. Immigrants learned that there were real costs involved in this favored social myth. Some responded optimistically to the pressure. Others did not. Their experience of life in a foreign land provided a 'family story' which embodies aspects of the Horatio Alger story. But the other side of the story, the struggle of immigrants in the face of difficult conditions in America, has remained a powerful undercurrent in American life.

The factors which drew people to settle in the United States have been thoughtfully mapped by historians: 'pull' factors such as economic betterment and opportunity, side by side with 'push' factors of economic hardship, political exclusion and persecution. What immigrants found in America, set out in the *Handbook*, was a society brimming with frontier opportunities. Advice was offered about keeping cows and sheep, and the harsh reality of living in a cabin 'of sods, or logs, or of canvas' was properly emphasized. Food on the frontier was likely to be rough and of poor quality, and immigrants would find themselves scorched by the prairie summer sun, and buried by the winter snows. 'Neighbors at first will be few and far apart' (p.127). Churches and schools would be built, neighbors would arrive; in time there would be a community (of sorts). The harshness of such a life had an appeal for some, especially those who felt hemmed in by the limited opportunity of life in Europe and who yearned for far horizons. The world of European peasants and laborers was harsh enough to make the hardships of the American west worth serious thought.

Consider two men who emigrated from central Europe in the late nineteenth century. Emanuel or Emil Brath was born in 1848 in the small village of Nieder-Soor, in the county of Trautenau, Germany (now part of the Czech Republic). Only the briefest outline of his life can be reconstructed. He married Paulina Beier in 1872 (she was then eighteen) and they emigrated to the even smaller township of Stetsonville, Wisconsin, where they had five children. Their son Joseph Albert Brath was born in Stetsonville in 1885. In 1909 Joseph Brath married Anna Gotz in Auburndale, some 46 miles distant.

Louis Gotz (Goetz appears as the family name in early records), a resourceful and hardworking young man, was born in Bohemia 1863. He attended common school and had completed a three-year apprenticeship as a blacksmith before accompanying his parents to America in 1881. He was eighteen. The family settled in Auburndale, Wood County, Wisconsin, where they bought a tract of forty acres of unimproved land, on which they built a log cabin. Monica Hilgardt, whom he had known in Bohemia, joined a sister in Auburndale. Monica and Louis were married in 1886. The first of their fifteen children, Anna, was born a year later. The young couple bought a tract of unimproved land two miles north of Auburndale and built a log cabin. Eventually their holding was enlarged to 150 acres of farmland. A history of Wood County noted that that Louis Gotz, a progressive Republican, was one of Auburndale's 'foremost citizens' His family attended St. Mary's Catholic Church in Auburndale, located on Main Street, between Schultz Ave and Fuehrer Ave.

Their oldest daughter Anna was married in October 1909. The bridegroom, Joseph Brath, was twenty-four and appears as a farmer on their wedding certificate. Anna was a 'Housekeeper'. The family settled in Miles City, Montana, where their daughter Polly was born in 1916. By 1920 Brath was back in Auburndale, keeping a hotel. He died in Miles City in 1930. Anna remarried. Their daughter Polly, my mother-in-law, graduated from the Michael Reese School, of Nursing in Chicago in 1936.

The Brath family from Germany and the Gotz family from Bohemia remained Roman Catholics, and German-speaking, throughout their lives. When in 1888 a Republican governor of Wisconsin put forward legislation which would, in effect, have banned the German language in all state schools, the German community was in an uproar. Traditionally Germans in the midwest voted Democrat, and though the 'Bennett Law' was never activated it soured relations across religious and political lines. Did a Republican like Louis Gotz, and (one assumes) Democrats like the Braths, look at each other differently over such an issue? Both families preferred rural, small-town life, whether in Bohemia, Wisconsin or Montana. It was the dominant pattern of their lives. When they had money, they bought land. They wanted something rather like what they had known. They were both cautious, conservative families, seeking to find what felt familiar to them.

'The moral of our long dissertation', conclude the authors of the *Handbook*, 'is that with health, industry, enterprise, and economy a man can achieve a competence almost anywhere' (p.153). That was the Poor Richard message, and Horatio Alger could not have stated it more clearly. To find good land, and settle in a decent small-town; to marry a hard-working man; to find a devoted wife; to have a large family: that was their opportunity and their hope, and they found it in a hundred places like Stetsonville, Auburndale and Miles City.

Eric Homberger
Professor Emeritus of American Studies
University of East Anglia, Norwich

Suggested further reading:
Willa Cather, *O Pioneers* (1913), *The Song of the Lark* (1915), *My Ántonia* (1918).
Michael Lesy, *Wisconsin Death Trip* (1973).

PREFACE.

The Manual which is now offered has thus far been published solely as an accompaniment to *Watson's New Railroad Map of the United States*, and has never been offered to the general trade, though often sought for. The Publisher has at length determined to comply with the demand for its more general circulation, and adapt it to a new class of customers, those who are seeking homes for themselves in our country, and especially in the West and South.

We have added all the necessary information in regard to the landed States and Territories, to enable any intending settler to decide which is the best region for him to select, how he may get there most comfortably and economically, what steps he must take to secure a perfect title to his lands, and what are in each case the best crops for him to raise, or the best business to pursue.

No Manual has ever contained a quarter of the information here offered, for the intending settler, or for the enterprising mechanic or working man, who desires to make himself a new home beyond the Mississippi; and as pains have been taken to make it perfectly accurate, and neither publisher or any one else concerned has any axes to grind, it may be received as standard authority in all the matters of which it treats.

THE PUBLISHER, 1880

CONTENTS.

RUTHERFORD B. HAYES

THE GENERAL GOVERNMENT.

ITS PRINCIPAL DEPARTMENTS–OFFICERS OF THE
CABINET, THE ARMY AND NAVY–DIPLOMATIC
RELATIONS

PRESIDENT.

Rutherford B. Hayes, of Ohio. Term expires March 4, 1881.

The President is chosen by Electors, who are elected by the People, each State having as many as it has Senators and Representatives in Congress. He holds office four years; is Commander-in-Chief of the Army and Navy of the United States; has power to grant pardons and reprieves for offenses against the United States; makes treaties, by and with the advice and consent of the Senate; nominates, and, with the consent of the Senate, appoints, all Cabinet, Diplomatic, Judicial and Executive officers; has power to convene Congress, or the Senate only; communicates with Congress by message at every session; receives all Foreign Ministers; takes care that the laws are faithfully executed, and the public business transacted. Salary $50,000 a year.

VICE–PRESIDENT

William A. Wheeler, of New York. Term expires March 4, 1881.

Is chosen by the Electors at the same time, and in the same manner as the President; is President of the Senate, and has the casting vote therein. In case of the death, resignation, disability or removal of the President, his powers and duties devolve upon the Vice-President for the residue of his term. In cases of vacancy, where the Vice-President succeeds to the Presidential office, the President of the Senate becomes *ex-officio* Vice-President. Salary $10,000 a year.

THE STATE DEPARTMENT

Preserves the public archives, records, laws, documents and treaties, and supervises their publication; conducts all business and correspondence arising out of Foreign Relations; makes out and records passports, commissions, etc.

Department Officers — Salary.

	Salary.
Secretary of State – Wm. M. Evarts, of New York	$8,000
Assistant Secretary – Fred. W. Seward, of New York	$3,500
Second Assistant Secretary – Wm. Hunter, of Rhode Island	$3,500
Third " " – Charles Payson, of Mass	$3,500

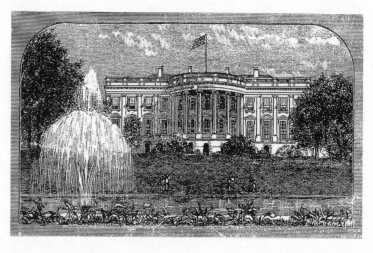

THE TREASURY DEPARTMENT

Has charge of all moneys paid into the United States Treasury, and general supervision of the fiscal transactions of the Government, the collection of revenue, the auditing and payment of accounts, and other disbursements; supervises the execution of the laws relating to Commerce and Navigation of the United States, the Revenues and Currency, the Coast Survey, the Mint and Coinage, the Light-

House Establishment, the construction of Marine Hospitals, Custom-Houses, &c.

Principal Department Officers

	Salary.
Secretary of the Treasury – John Sherman, of Ohio	$8,000
Assistant Secretary – John B. Hawley, of Illinois	$4,500
" – Henry F. French, of Massachusetts	$4,500
Supervising Architect – James G. Hill, of Massachusetts	$4,500
Treasurer of United States – James Gilfillan, of Connecticut	$6,000

THE WAR DEPARTMENT

Has charge of business growing out of military affairs, keeps the records of the army, issues commissions, directs the movement of troops, superintends their payment, stores, clothing, arms and equipments and ordnance, constructs fortifications, and conducts works of military engineering, and river and harbor improvements.

Principal Department Officers

	Salary.
Secretary of War – Geo. W. McCeary, of Iowa	$8,000
Chief Clerk – H. T. Crosby, of Pennsylvania	$2,500
Inspector General— Brevet Major General Randolph B. Marcy, of Mass	
Jndge Advocate General—Colonel Joseph McKee Dunn, of Indiana	
Adjutant General—Brevet Major General E. D. Townsend, of D. C.	

THE NAVY DEPARTMENT

Has charge of the Naval Establishment and all business connected therewith, issues Naval Commissions, instructions and orders, supervises the enlistment and discharge of seamen, the Marine Corps, the construction of Navy Yards and Docks, the construction and equipment of Vessels, the purchase of provisions, stores, clothing and ordnance, the conduct of surveys and hydrographical operations.

Principal Department Officers	Salary.
Secretary of the Navy – Richard W. Thompson, of Indiana	$8,000
Chief Clerk – John W. Hogg, of District of Columbia	$2,500
Superintendent of Naval Observatory – Rear-Admiral John Rodgers	
Hydrographic Office – Captain S. R. Franklin	
Superintendent National Almanac – Prof. Simon Newcomb	
Commander of Marine Corps – Colonel C. G. McCawley	
Chief Signal Officer – Commodore John C. Beaumont	

DEPARTMENT OF THE INTERIOR

Has charge of the survey, management, sales and grants of Public Lands, the examination of Pension and Bounty Land claims, the management of Indian affairs, the examination of Inventions and award of Patents, the taking of Censuses, the management of Government mines, the erection of Public Buildings, and the construction of wagon roads to the Pacific.

Principal Department Officers	Salary.
Secretary of the Interior – Carl Schurz, of Missouri	$8,000
Assistant Secretary – Charles F. Gorham, of Mich	$3,500
General Land Office – James A. Williamson, of Iowa, Commissioner	$4,000
Indian Office – Ezra A. Hayt, of New York, Commissioner	$4,500
Pension Office – John A. Bentley, of Wisconsin, "	$3,600
Patent Office – Halbert E. Paine, " "	$4,500
Bureau of Education – John Eaton, of Tenn., "	$3,000

THE POST OFFICE DEPARTMENT

Has charge of the Postal System, the establishment and discontinuance of Post Offices, appointment of Postmasters, contracts for carrying the mails, the Dead Letter Office, maintains an inspection to prevent frauds, etc.

Principal Department Officers	Salary.
Postmaster-General – David M. Key, of Tennessee:	$8,000
Appointment Office—1st Assistant P. M. General,	
Jas. M. Tyner, Ind	$3,500
General Superintendent R. R. Mail Service—W. B. Thompson,	
of Ohio	$3,000
Auditor Railroad Accounts—Theophilus French	$2,000
Topographer—W. F. Nicholson, of D. C	

DEPARTMENT OF JUSTICE

The Attorney-General, who is the head of this department, is the legal adviser of the President and heads of departments, examines titles, applications for pardons, and judicial and legal appointments, conducts and argues suits in which Government is concerned, etc.

Principal Department Officers.	Salary.
Attorney-General – Charles Devens, of Mass	$8,000
Assistant Attorney-General – Edwin B. Smith, of Maine	$5,000
Assistant Attorney-General – Thomas Simons, of New York	$5,000
Solicitor-General – Samuel F. Phillips, of North Carolina	$7,000
Solicitor of Internal Revenue – C. Chesley, of New Hampshire	$4,500
Solicitor of the Treasury – Kenneth Raynor, of N. Carolina	$4,500

THE JUDICIARY

Supreme Court of the United States

Appointed.		Age	Salary
1874.—Morrison R. Waite, of Ohio.	Chief Justice.	63	$10,500
1880.—Geo. F. Edmunds, of Vermont.....	...Asso. Jus.	68	$10,000
1858.—Nathan Clifford, Portland, Maine	..........”	75	$10,000
1862.—Noah H. Swayne, Columbus, Ohio,	..........”	74	$10,000
1862.—Samuel F. Miller, Keokuk, Iowa	..........”	63	$10,000
1863.—Stephen J. Field, California,	..........”	62	$10,000
1870.—Joseph P. Bradley, New Jersey	..........”	66	$10,000
1870.—William Strong, Pennsylvania,	..........”	70	$10,000
1877.—John M. Harlan, Kentucky	..........”	64	$10,000

The Court holds one general term annually, at Washington, D.C., commencing on the first Monday in December.

THE LEGISLATIVE BRANCH

The National Legislature consists of a Senate of two members from each State, making the full Senate now consist of seventy-six members, and a House of Representatives, now having two hundred and ninety-three members. Senators are chosen by the Legislatures of their several States, for a term of six years, either by concurrent vote or by joint ballot, as the State may prescribe. The members of the House of Representatives are usually elected by a plurality vote in districts of each State, whose bounds are prescribed by the Legislature, for the term of two years.

The Constitution requires nine years' citizenship to qualify for admission to the Senate, and seven years to the House of Representatives. The members of each House receive a salary of $5,000 per annum, and actual mileage at twenty cents per mile. For each day's absence, except when caused by sickness, $8 per diem is deducted from the salary. The Speaker of the House of Representatives receives $10,000.

Presidents under the Federal Constitution

Names.	Inaugurated.	Born.	Age at Inaugu-ration.	Years in office.	Died.	Age at Death
1. George Washington, of Virginia.........	April 30, 1789	1732	57	8	Dec. 14, 1799	68
2. John Adams, of Massachusetts...........	Mar. 4—1797	1735	62	4	July 4—1826	91
3. Thomas Jefferson, of Virginia............	Mar. 4—1801	1743	58	8	July 4—1826	83
4. James Madison, of Virginia..............	Mar. 4—1809	1751	58	8	June 28, 1836	85
5. James Monroe, of Virginia...............	Mar. 4—1817	1759	58	8	July 4—1831	72

No.	Name	Term	Born	Age	Term yrs	Died	Age
6.	John Quincy Adams, of Mass............	Mar. 4—1825	1767	58	4	Feb. 23, 1848	80
7.	Andrew Jackson, of Tennessee............	Mar. 4—1829	1767	62	8	June 8—1845	78
8.	Martin Van Buren, of New York........	Mar. 4—1837	1782	55	4	July 24, 1862	79
9.	William Henry Harrison, of Ohio........	Mar. 4—1841	1773	68	—	April 4, 1841	68
10.	John Tyler, of Virginia, *Vice-President,* succeeded President Harrison who died April 4, 1841.........	Apr. 4—1841	1790	57	4	Jan. 17, 1862	72
11.	James K Polk, of Tennesse................	Mar. 4—1845	1795	49	4	June 15, 1849	54
12.	Zachary Taylor, of Louisiana............	Mar. 4—1849	1784	65	1	July 9—1850	66
13.	Millard Fillmore, of N. Y., *Vice-President,* succeeded Pres. Taylor, who died July 9, 1850.............	July. 9—1850	1800	50	3	Mar. 8—1874	74
14.	Franklin Pierce, of N. Hampshire......	Mar. 4—1853	1804	49	4	Oct. 8—1869	65
15.	James Buchanan, of Pennsylvania.....	Mar. 4—1857	1791	65	4	June 1—1869	77
16.	Abraham Lincoln, of Illinois..............	Mar. 4—1861	1809	52	4	April 15, 1865	50
17.	Andrew Johnson, *Vice-President,* succeeded President Lincoln, who was assassinated April 14, 1865.........	Apr. 15—1865	1808	57	4	July 31, 1875	67
18.	Ulysses S. Grant, of Illinois..............	Mar. 4—1869	1822	47	8		
19.	Rutherford B. Hayes, of Ohio.............	Mar. 4—1877	1822	55			

Vice-Presidents.

Names.	Inaugurated.	Born.	Died.
1. John Adams, of Massachusetts...........	1789	1735	1826
2. Thomas Jefferson, of Virginia.............	1797	1743	1826
3. Aaron Burr, of New York.....................	1801	1756	1836
4. George Clinton, of New York..............	1805	1739	1812
5. Elbridge Gerry, of Massachusetts.......	1813	1744	1814
6. Daniel D. Tompkins, of New York......	1817	1744	1825
7. John C. Calhoun, of South Carolina...	1825	1782	1850
8. Martin Van Buren, of New York.........	1833	1782	1862
9. Richard M. Johnson, of Kentucky......	1837	1780	1850
10. John Tyler, of Virginia.........................	1841	1790	1862
11. George M. Dallas, of Pennsylvania.....	1845	1792	1865
12. Millard Fillmore, of New York............	1849	1800	1874
13. William R. King, of Alabama..............	1853	1786	1853
14. John C. Breckenridge, of Kentucky....	1857	1821	1875
15. Hannibal Hamlin, of Maine.................	1861	1809	
16. Andrew Johnson, of Tennessee...........	1865	1808	1875
17. Schuyler Colfax, of Indiana.................	1869	1823	
18. Henry Wilson, of Massachusetts.........	1873	1812	1875
19. William A. Wheeler, of New York........	1877		

Chief Justices of the Supreme Court of the United States.

Name.	State.	Term of Service.	Born.	Died.
John Jay	New York	1789—1795	1745	1829
John Rutledge	South Carolina	1795—1795	1739	1800
Oliver Ellsworth	Connecticut	1796—1801	1752	1807
John Marshall	Virginia	1801—1836	1755	1836
Roger B. Taney	Maryland	1836—1864	1777	1864
Salmon P. Chase	Ohio	1864—1873	1808	1873
Morrison R. Waite	Ohio	1874—......	1825	....

DEBT OF VARIOUS ADMINISTRATIONS
SINCE 1793

Washington's First Term	1793	$80,352,636
John Adam's	1801	$82,038,050
Jefferson's First Term	1805	$82,312,150
" Second Term	1809	$57,023,192
Madison's First Term	1813	$59,962,827
" Second Term	1817	$123,491,965
Monroe's First Term	1821	$89,987,427
John Quincy Adams	1829	$59,421,413
Jackson's First Term	1833	$7,001,022
Van Buren	1841	$6,488,784
Tyler	1845	$17,093,794
Polk	1849	$64,704,693
Fillmore	1853	$67,340,620
Pierce	1857	$29,060,387
Buchanan	1861	$90,867,828
Lincoln	1865	$2,682,593,026
Johnson	1869	$2,491,399,904
Grant	1871	$2,320,708,846
Hayes	1878	£2,042,037,129

RATES OF DOMESTIC POSTAGE

Letters

The standard weight is ½ oz. avoirdupois.

Single-rate letter, throughout the United States – 3 cts.

For each additional ½ oz. – 3 "

Drop letters, for local delivery, single rate – 2 "

Postal card, throughout the United States – 1 "

These postages must be prepaid by stamps. Properly certified letters of soldiers and sailors will be forwarded without pre-payment.

Postal Cards

The object of the postal card is to facilitate letter correspondence, at a reduced rate of postage, of short communications, either printed or written in pencil or ink. They may be used for orders, invitations, notices, receipts, price-lists, and other requirements of business and social life.

The postage of one cent each is paid by the stamp impressed on these cards, and no further payment is required. No card is a "postal card" except such as are issued by the Post Office Department.

The following articles are unmailable:
Packages containing liquids, poisons, glass, explosive chemicals, live animals, sharp-pointed instruments, flour, sugar, or any other matter liable to deface the mail, or injure any one connected with the service. All letters upon the envelope of which indecent, lewd, obscene, or lascivious delineations or language may be written or printed, or disloyal devices printed or engraved. Also, all obscene, lewd, or lascivious books, pamphlets, pictures, papers, prints, or other publications of an indecent character.

RAILROAD STATISTICS

Mileage of railroads in operation, and annual increase, 1830-1878. [From *Poor's Manual of the Railroads of the United States.*]

Years.	Miles in Operati'n.	Annual Increase of Mileage.	Years.	Miles in Operati'n	Annual Increase of Mileage.
1830.....	23	....	1855.....	18,374	1,654
1831.....	95	72	1856.....	22,016	3,642
1832.....	229	134	1857.....	24,503	2,487
1833.....	380	151	1858.....	26,968	2,465
1834.....	633	253	1859.....	28,789	1,821
1835.....	1 098	465	1860.....	30,635	1,846
1836.....	1,273	175	1861.....	31,286	651
1837.....	1,497	224	1862.....	32,120	834
1838.....	1,913	416	1863.....	33,170	1,050
1839.....	2,302	389	1864.....	33,908	738

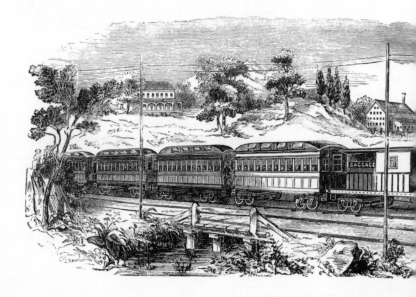

1840.....	2,818	516	1865.....	35,085	1,177
1841.....	3,535	717	1866.....	36,827	1,742
1842.....	4,026	491	1867.....	39,276	2,449
1843.....	4,185	159	1868.....	42,255	2,979
1844.....	4,377	192	1869.....	47,208	4,953
1845.....	4,633	256	1870.....	52,898	5,690
1846.....	4,930	297	1871.....	60,568	7,670
1847.....	5,598	668	1872.....	66,735	6,167
1848.....	5,996	398	1873.....	70,840	4,105
1849.....	7,365	1,369	1874.....	72,741	1,901
1850.....	9,021	1,656	1875.....	74,658	1,917
1851.....	10,982	1,961	1876.....	77,514	2,856
1852.....	12,908	1,926	1877.....	79,795	2,281
1853.....	15,360	2,452	1878.....	82,483	2,281
1854.....	16,720	1,360			

It is estimated that there are 1,900 miles of railroad track, in double, treble or quadruple tracks, sidings, etc., making the total length in single track, January 1, 1878, 98,208 miles, and January 1,1879, about 101,000 miles. The mileage of 1878 is 2,688 against 2,281 in 1877.

Mileage of new railroads constructed in each state and territory for five years. [From *The Railway Age.*]

States, & c.	1874.	1875.	1876.	1877.	1878.
Alabama	18	......	......	1½	22
Alaska	......	......	......	....	......
Arizona	......	......	......	....	30
Arkansas	18	38½	49	......	7
California	140½	185	344¾	235⅜	71½
Colorado	23	111½	154½	123½	193¼
Connecticut	......	21	7	3½	......
Dakota	......	......	......	......	15
Delaware	19	5	......	......	6
Florida	18	......	......	13	......
Georgia	5	4	42	......	62
Idaho	......	......	......	......	126
Illinois	231	200	58	55¼	103
Indiana	209½	109½	72¼	24	74
Indian Ter't'y	......	......	2	......	......
Iowa	48	84½	96¾	165½	255½
Kansas	61	......	76	86½	169¼
Kentucky	31¼	......	138	28¼	20
Louisiana	......	......	......	2	......
Maine	37½	10	20	......	......
Maryland	12	17	15	......	5½
Massachus'ts	27¾	36	5	17¼	6
Michigan	48	30	46	56	110½
Minnesota	36	......	34	204	338¼
Mississippi	27	......	10	......	26
Missouri	31	27	109½	36	209
Montana	......	......	......	......	......
Nebraska	......	22	52	69	55

Nevada	40	64	......	......	......
N. Hampshire	45	15½	9¼	18	35
New Jersey	39	72¼	84	81½	3
New Mexico	......	......	......	......	......
New York	125¼	206	69¾	151¾	129½
N. Carolina	68	13	43	27	16
Ohio	172½	26	275	269	97
Oregon	......	......	......	......	36
Pennsylvania	191½	136¾	90½	119¾	188½
Rhode Island	14	......	9	9⅜	......
S. Carolina	......	15	17	48¾	16½
Tennessee	......	......	7½	21¾	10
Texas	75	34½	387¾	168½	118½
Utah	59	27	......	20	......
Vermont	5	32	......	71	......
Virginia	70¾	......	10	16¾	16½
Washington T	6	......	......	52½	15
W. Virginia	......	......	......	20½	16½
Wisconsin	102	23	123¾	62	83¾
Wyoming Ter	......	......	......	5	......
Total	5,025	1,561	2,450	1,281	2,688

THE AMERICAN POPULATION.

EDUCATION – RELIGION – POPULATION – RACE –
CRIME – STATISTICS OF IMMIGRATION

EDUCATIONAL

The Educational condition of the United States, though not yet what we may hope it will be, is far in advance of that of any other nation. Some of the German States maintain a system of compulsory education, which ensures to every child a certain amount of intellectual training, but it is not so beneficial as our more free and practical system of education. In our country, up to the close of the late war, very few of the Southern States had any thorough system of primary education, and many of their secondary and higher schools, colleges and seminaries, were very superficial; but the last ten years has witnessed a great advance in these respects in those States, and the Northern States have made equally rapid progress.

The tables which follow, show that nearly 9,000,000 of our children – somewhat more than one-fifth of our entire population – are enrolled in our Public Schools; 246,654 in our secondary and special schools, the Universities and Colleges have 56,253 students, and the Scientific and Professional Schools 25,039, making a grand total of nearly 9,600,000 children and youth under instruction; more than 270,000 teachers are engaged in the work of instruction.

For the purposes of this education, the investment in real estate, appliances for teaching, and libraries, is over $314,000,000. No nation in the world can make such an exhibit as this, but we may fairly hope that another decade will show one-fourth of our population under instruction, with greatly increased facilities.

Statistics of the public schools of the United States for 1876.

STATES AND TERRITORIES.	School Age.	School Population.	Number enrolled in Public Schools.	Number of Teachers employed in Public School.	
				Male.	Female.
Alabama................	5 to 21	406,270	147,340	2,702	1,297
Arkansas...............	6..21	184,692	73,878	1,582	740
California..............	5..17	171,563	130,930	1,033	1,660
Colorado................	5..21	23,275	12,552	172	205
Connecticut...........	4..16	134,976	120,189	721	2,324
Delaware...............	5..21	47,825	19,881	(430)	
Florida..................	6..21	94,522	32,371	(796)	
Georgia.................	6..18	394,037	156,394	....	....
Illinois...................	6..21	958,003	687,446	9,288	12,330
Indiana.................	6..21	667,711	502,362	7,670	5,463
Iowa......................	5..21	533,903	384,012	6,500	11,645
Kansas..................	5..21	199,986	142,606	2,484	2,899
Kentucky..............	6..20	437,100	228,000	4,236	1,732
Louisiana..............	6..21	274,688	74,846	797	760
Maine....................	4..21	221,477	157,323	1,984	4,475
Maryland...............	5..20	276,120	142,992	1,129	1,594
Massachusetts......	5..15	294,708	302,118	1,169	8,047
Michigan...............	5..21	448,784	343,619	3,285	9,182
Minnesota.............	5..21	218,641	130,280	1,372	1,591
Missippi................	5..21	318,459	168,217	2,989	1,979
Missouri...............	5..21	738,431	394,780	5,904	3,747

Nebraska...............	5..21	80,122	55,423	1,504	1,587
Nevada.................	6..18	6,315	4,811	35	80
New Hampshire...	4..21	76,272	68,751	503	3,166
New Jersey............	5..18	312,694	191,731	946	2,307
New York...............	5..21	1,583,064	1,059,238	7,428	22,585
North Carolina.....	6..21	348,603	146,737	(2,690)	
Ohio.......................	6..21	1,017,726	712,129	12,306	10,186
Oregon...................	4..20	44,661	21,518	496	457
Pennsylvania........	6..21	1,222,697	890,073	8,585	11,295
Rhode Island.........	5..15	53,316	38,554	195	861
South Carolina.....	6..16	239,264	110,416	1,773	1,082
Tennessee.............	6..18	426,612	199,058	3,125	1 085
Texas.....................	5..20	313,061	184,705	(4,030)	
Vermont.................	5..21	89,541	78,139	667	3,739
Virginia.................	5..21	482,789	184,486	2,711	1,551
West Virginia........	6..21	179,897	115,300	2,677	784
Wisconsin..............	4..20	461,829	279,854	(9,451)	
Totals		13,983,634	8,693,289	(247,468)	
Arizona..................	6..21	2,508	568	6	8
Dakota...................	5..21	8,343	4,428	54	154
Dist. of Columbia	6..17	31,671	18,785	22	271
Idaho......................	5..21	4,020	3,270	....	....
Montana................	4..21	3,822	2,215	43	56
New Mexico..........	7..18	29,312	5,151	132	15
Utah.......................	4..16	35,696	19,278	220	238
Washington...........	4..21	8,350	6,699	(2	20)
Wyoming...............	5..20	1,095	1,222	7	16
Indian....................	6..16	....	3,754	....	....
Total		124,817	77,922	(1,839)	
Grand Totals		14,108,451	8,771,211	(249,307)	

STATISTICS OF THE PUBLIC SCHOOLS OF THE UNITED STATES, JAN., 1876.

STATES and TERRITORIES.	Average Monthly Salary of Teachers.		Annual income of the Public Schools	Annual Expenditures of Public Schools.				
	Male.	Female.		Sites, Buildings, Libraries, Furniture and apparatus.	Salaries of Superintendents.	Salaries of Teachers.	Miscellaneous.	Total Expenditures.
Alabama..........	$(27.	20)	$553,014	$100	34,187	$489,492	....	523,779
Arkansas..........	....	....	789,536	54,912	24,100	259,747	....	750,000
California..........	84.93	68.01	3,390,359	465,955	43,622	1,810,479	381,803	2,701,863
Colorado..........	60.00	48.00	254,679	76,215	7,500	102,783	31,815	218,313
Connecticut..........	70.05	37.35	1,592,749	220,942	20,000	1,057,242	254,399	1,552,583
Delaware..........	(28.	00)	192,735	....	....	....	....	....
Florida..........	50.00	30.00	188,952	....	15,600	....	....	107,724
Georgia..........	....	....	435,319	....	....	....	....	....
Illinois..........	48.21	33 32	8,268,540	1,090,574	....	5,326,780	971,854	8,268,540
Indiana..........	65.00	40.00	5,041,517	700,000	50,000	2,830,747	949,457	4,530,204

State								
Iowa	36.68	28.33	5,035,498	1,114,68??	......	2,598,440	892,626	4,605,749
Kansas	33.98	27.25	1,042,298	182,886	34,100	689,907	113,208	1,020,101
Kentucky	(49.	40)	1,438,436	111,406	......	......	......	1,559,452
Louisiana	37.00	37.00	699,665	60,182	24,000	573,144	42,339	699,665
Maine	37.00	18.00	1,313,303	110,725	29,668	1,046,766	126,144	1,313,303
Maryland	41.73	41.73	1,376,046	272,539	25,440	1,035,755	307,313	1,641,047
Massachusetts	88.37	35.35	6,410,514	1,533,142	......	......	......	7,000,000
Michigan	51.29	28.19	4,173,551	571,109	......	1,950,928	994,745	3,516,782
Minnesota	41.36	28.91	1,861,158	208,030	......	702,662	247,755	1,158,447
Mississippi	55.47	55.47	1,110,248	55,000	48,650	856,950	80,000	1,040,600
Missouri	38.00	29.50	3,013,595	......	......	......	......	3,000,000
Nebraska	38.60	33.10	292,475	327,406	18,916	414,827	167,039	928,188
Nevada	(100.	56)	146,181	22,723	......	83,548	18,030	124,301
New Hampshire	42.61	25.54	621,649	264,244	......	424,889	53,721	742,854
New Jersey	67.65	37.75	2,311,465	549,619	28,770	1,731,816	30,780	2,340,985
New York	(58.	36)	11,601,256	2,181,927	......	7,849,667	1,569,662	11,601,256
North Carolina	30.00	25.00	500,000	15,100	......	158,129	8,445	300,000
Ohio	60.00	44.00	8,711,411	1,313,515	158,773	4,787,964	1,391,704	7,651,956
Oregon	51.45	45.50	204,760	3,125	2,000	......	......	215,707
Pennsylvania	41.07	34.09	8,798,816	2,059,465	106,050	4,640,825	2,557,587	9,363,927

Rhode Island	58.18	46.17	761,796	275,835	11,681	383,284	77,059	764,643
South Carolina	31.64	29.21	489,542	22,222		369,685	34,554	426,461
Tennessee	30.85	30.85	740,316	44,406	19,385	582,918	42,420	703,358
Texas	(53.	00)	244,879	60,081	9,233	630,334	26,588	726,236
Vermont	45.62	25.65	516,252	89,789	12,643	440,536	82,089	625,057
Virginia	33.52	28.71	1,215,353	97,278	48,668	726,300	151,150	1,023,396
West Virginia	35.03	30.77	753,477	123,844	2,500	541,359	47,457	715,160
Wisconsin	50.83	33.28	2,308,187	371,496	50,000	1,350,884	241,777	2,066,375
Totals			88,399,237	14,710,475	825,486	46,448,787	11,893,524	5,526,912
Arizona	100.00	100.00	28,759					24,151
Dakota	35.00	25.00	32,602	9,985		18,046	4,572	32,603
Dist. of Columbia	113.00	75.00	517,610	61,123	9,520	209,368	86,568	366,579
Idaho	55.00	55.00	22,497					17,2?0
Montana	65.00	57.00	31,821	28,726	4,500	33,921		67,147
New Mexico			25,473			15,432	3,458	18,890
Utah	47.00	23.00	130,799	49,568	3,450	130,800		183,818
Washington						54,720		54,720
Wyoming						16,400		16,400
Indian			99,929					99,000
Total			889,490	149,402	17,470	578,687	94,598	886,528
Grand Totals			89,288,727	14,859,877	842,956	47,027,474	11,988,122	86,407,440

Secondary Instruction

Some schools of secondary or superior instruction, under a variety of names, form the connecting links between the public school and the college or university. Some of these are private schools but somewhat permanent in character; they may be schools for boys, or for girls, or both; others rank as academies, high schools or seminaries; others still, are preparatory schools for the college course; others still as schools of superior instruction for women, Female Seminaries, Colleges, Academies, or Collegiate Institutes. Still another class, are Commercial or Business Colleges. There are also Normal Schools or Colleges, sometimes private, sometimes State or City institutions, intended for training teachers – and schools of special instruction for deaf mutes, blind, feeble minded, orphans and juvenile offenders. The character of these schools is so diverse that we cannot bring them under a table, showing the number in each State, but we give below the aggregate number of each class in the entire country, with such particulars as can be collected concerning them, premising that a considerable number are not reported in any year.

Scientific and Professional Schools

The Scientific Schools are of two classes. Those organized under the law making grants of land to Agricultural Colleges (and receiving the avails of these grants) and those endowed by State or private munificence. The Theological Seminaries and institutions can be classed under a single head, though only some are connected with Colleges or Universities; some have a course of classical study, and others are confined to theological studies exclusively. The Law Schools come under a single head, but the Medical Schools are divided into Regular Homoeopathic and Eclectic, and the Dental and Pharmaceutical Schools are also classed with them. We give herewith such statistics as can be obtained of all these Scientific and Professional Schools.

In most of the Theological Schools, the tuitions provided for by endowment and is free. The Scholarships of the Scientific Schools cover the tuition; there are also free scholarships in some of the Medical Schools – usually the result of State grants.

CLASSES OF SCHOOLS.	No. Schools in U.S.	Teachers. No. Male	Teachers. No. Fem.	Number of Pupils. Total	No. Male Pupils.	No. Female Pupils.	Income from all Sources.	No. of Volumes in Libraries.
Schools & Acad. Boys.	215	830	152	15,793	15,676	117	$1,144,632	114,816
Schools & Acad. Girls.	311	510	1,943	22,375	45	21,918	900,125	122,885
Schools, Boys & Girls.	617	1,239	1,407	70,067	36,978	33,089	1,255,166	266,316
Preparatory Schools.	102	(7	46)	12,954	(12.	954)	456,776	86,488
Schools, Acads. Sem. Col. &Col. Ins. for superior instruction of women	222	585	1,592	23,975	....	23,975	1,259,411	217,023
Normal Schools & Col.	137	(1.0	31)	29,105	12,924	16,181	684,071	96,103
Com. & Business Col.	131	(5	94)	26,109	(26,	100)	....	19,699
Kindergarten	95	(2	16)	2,809	(2,	809)	....	....
Special instruction —								
Schools for Deaf Mutes.	41	(2	94)	5,087	2,795	2,292	1,144,044	29,640
Schools for the Blind.	29	(4	98)	2,054	(2,	054)	866,411	11,498
Schools, feeble minded, idiotic, & c	9	(3.1	71)	1,372	816	556	242,514	....
Reform Schools	47	367	311	10,670	8,111	2,559	1,145,315	??85
Orphan Asylums,. Soldier's Or. Homes, Infant Asylums & Indus. Schools.	207	(1.3	28)	24,584	10,656	13,928	3,036,453	4?,020
Grand Totals	2,163	(14.0	60)	246,654	(246,	654)	12,132,913	1,145,671

CLASSES OF SCHOOLS OR INSTITUTIONS IN UNITED STATES.	Number of Schools.	Number of Professors or Instructors.	Whole Number of Students.	Number of Male Students.	Number of Female Students.	Income from all Sources.	Number of Scholarships.	Volumes in Library.
I. SCIENTIFIC SCHOOLS								
A—Schools endowed from Agricultural gr'nt	43	539	4,919		(4,919)	642,345	1,250	93,501
B—Not thus endowed	31	219	2,238		(2,238)	228,338	216	60,198
II. THEOLOGICAL SCH'LS	123	615	5,234		(5,234)	....	....	599,177
III. LAW SCHOOLS	43	224	2,677		(2,677)	70,639	....	62,311
IV. MEDICAL SCHOOLS								
A—Regular Practice.	65	809	7,518		(7,518)	308,721	....	57,390
B—Homeopathic	11	136	664		(664)	46,174	....	4,180
C—Eclectic	4	36	398		(398)	25,428	....	1,400
Dental Schools	12	135	469		(469)	49,238	....	1,513
Schools of Pharmacy	14	56	922		(922)	26,511	....	7,760
Totals	346	2,769	25,039		(25,039)	1,397,394		877,430

In most of the Theological Schools, the tuition is provided for by endowment and is free. The Scholarships of the Scientific Schools cover the tuition; there are also free scholarships in some of the Medical Schools — usually the result of State grants.

STATISTICS OF UNIVERSITIES AND COLLEGES IN THE UNITED STATES IN 1876.

STATES.	No. of Universities & Colleges.	Whole No. Professors and Instructors.	Whole number of Students.	Income from all sources.	Amount of Scholarship Funds.	Number of Volumes in Libraries.
Alabama..............	4	49	304	81,500	....	14,300
Arkansas.............	4	16	305	7,250	....	400
California............	13	179	2,334	471,278	....	46,605
Connecticut........	3	57	847	136,504	60,000	141,000
Colorado.............	2	7	69	....	....	....
Delaware.............	1	7	40	9,000	....	7,200
Georgia...............	6	47	714	68,500	300	35,900
Illinois.................	26	342	4,766	219,923	55,500	112,543
Indiana...............	19	189	3,464	138,483	40,750	84,317
Iowa....................	18	203	3,864	133,699	38,032	42,714
Kansas................	6	41	417	36,996	....	7,708
Kentucky............	14	106	1,853	93,427	100,000	45,500
Louisiana............	6	45	356	14,849	....	21,050

Maine..................	3	32	383	69,400	85,060	50,695
Maryland............	8	125	917	272,788	....	45,705
Massachusetts....	7	132	1,763	352,082	681,258	271,584
Michigan.............	8	115	2,151	169,603	85,000	41,375
Minnesota...........	3	44	486	40,459	3,000	15,158
Mississippi..........	4	31	363	38,400	....	11,452
Missouri..............	20	251	2,846	259,127	75,000	77,545
Nebraska............	3	22	306	31,092	....	3,350
Nevada................	1	1	31	....	....	....
New Hampshire	1	37	357	36,000	100,000	57,000
New Jersey.........	4	54	805	102,737	92,185	59,414
New York............	26	486	5,952	1,095,452	420,392	240,832
North Carolina...	7	50	859	45,630	....	57,000
Ohio.....................	33	299	5,824	247,917	218,612	158,465
Oregon................	6	39	927	33,726	67,000	8,381
Pennsylvania......	29	354	4,124	379,768	72,000	189,698
Rhode Island......	1	15	255	74,308	57,725	45,000
South Carolina...	6	40	679	75,148	48,600	60,250
Tennessee...........	21	171	2,982	116,102	24,000	40,220
Texas...................	12	86	1,715	57,460	31,200	16,561
Vermont..............	3	22	194	23,181	64,500	32,921
Virginia...............	8	80	1,417	84,658	92,485	117,180
West Virginia......	3	27	353	39,760	....	11,230
Wisconsin...........	10	133	2,101	194,0??2	15,000	42,113
District of Columbia............	4	54	451	529	....	50,850
New Mexico........	1	8	93	9,817	....	....
Utah.....................	1	8	291	6,171	....	2,394
Washington Territory.............	1	3	56	....	....	500
Totals	356	4,007	56,253	5,257,836	2,527,649	2,256,110

RELIGIOUS STATISTICS OF THE USA

RELIGIOUS STATISTICS OF THE UNITED STATES IN 1878-9.

DENOMINATIONS & SECTS.	Archbishops Bis, Supts. & c	Clergymen.	Churches, Congregat'ns and Parishes	Communicants, or Memb'rs of Churches, Cong's, or Parishes.	Adherent Population.	Additions to Church Membership within the Year.	Sunday Schools.	Newsp'ers & Periodic'ls of Denom's.
Roman Catholic	66	5,548	8,170	3,970,000	6,078,000	....	....	35
Methodist Episcopal Church	11	11,303	17,337	1,487,177	6,692,296	78,778	19,961	48
" South	7	3,721	7,543	765 337	3,444,293	42,346	7,947	23
United Brethren in Christ	3	1,952	4,078	143,881	647,627	7,805	2,854	6
Other Methodists, incl. Col'd	25	6,495	9,586	799,038	3,596,052	8,419	10,447	22
Free-Will, or Free Baptists	......	1,367	1,993	75,826	338,413	8,127	....	5
Regular Baptists	......	14,954	24,499	2,102,034	9,459,153	102,736	12,629	52
Disciples	......	2,371	3,893	397,246	1,787,607	6,183	2,981	26
Menn'te, Tunkers Winebr'ns	......	3,688	4,031	410,600	1,847,700	65,000	....	6
7 Day, 6 Princ'l & other Bapt's	......	769	908	71,500	321,525	....	....	3
Presbyt'n Ch. Un. Gen. Assm	......	4,901	5,269	567,855	2,555,347	11,610	....	......
Presbyterian Church South	......	1,117	1,873	114,578	515,601	2,028	....	8

Denomination								
Refm'd Presbyter'ns, 4 Sects	......	306	322	28,069	126,310	873	......	2
United Presbyterians	......	647	661	78,048	351,216	1,259	709	3
Cumberland Presbyterians	......	1,312	2,347	106,253	478,012	3,583	587	3
Refm'd Ch. in U. S., late Ger	......	447	1,099	87,871	395,420	1,312	998	12
Refm'd Ch. in Amer. late Dut'h	......	543	503	79,413	357,358	1,004	648	3
Congregationalists	......	3,496	3,620	365,447	1,644,511	14,789	......	18
Protestant Episcopal Church	63	3,204	3,002	314,367	1,414,650	26,713	2,816	14
Reformed Episcopal Church	4	64	61	5,808	26,136	1,216	......	2
Lutherans	......	2,795	4,982	696,420	3,133,890	96,095	......	48
United Brethren—Morav'ns	5	98	75	9,212	40,954	913	......	3
Unitarians	......	401	358	31,780	143,100	......	......	5
Christian Connect'n, 3 Sects	......	1,271	1,461	98,640	447,300	......	......	6
Universalists	......	711	737	45,218	201,200	......	661	12
Friends—Orthodox	......	......	542	60,128	270,576	1,092	......	2
Friends—Hicksite & Progres	......	......	......	40,000	180,000	......	......	2
New Jerus. or Swedenborg'n	......	81	90	7,450	31,000	......	......	9
Jews	......	185	220	57,500	112,540	......	......	10
Mormons	155	735	......	120,000	155,000	......	......	8
Spiritualists	......	......	......	30,000	155,000	......	......	10
Minor Sects not included abv	......	3?70	425	50,000	150,000	......	......	6
Deist, Atheist, Rad. or Liberal	......	......	......	......	150,000	......	......	5

The above table has been prepared with great care, and in all cases from the latest authorities. The sittings, where not given by the Church authorities, are calculated from the same ratios as the table of denominations in the United States Census; and the adherent population on the ratio of 4½ adherents to each communicant, which long observation has proved to be more nearly accurate, than that of 5 to 1 usually employed. The only exceptions to this ratio, and those made for reasons which are obvious to all, are the Roman Catholic, the Jews, Mormons, and a few minor sects grouped together. In all these the members in full communion, or openly declared such, constitute a very large proportion of those who adhere to them—usually at least one half. The increase in the amount and value of Church property has been very great within the past ten years; and the recent decline in value of real estate has been in most cases more than made good by the erection of new churches and manses. It will be seen that the present estimated value is nearly $477,000,000.

CENSUS OF 1870

POPULATION OF THE UNITED STATES–GENERAL NATIVITY AND FOREIGN PARENTAGE.

[From the Report of the Superintendent of the Census.]

STATES AND TERRITORIES.	1870.		
	Total population.	Native born.	Foreign born.
Total U. States.......	38,558,371	32,991,142	5,567,229
Total States............	38,115,641	32,642,612	5,473,029
Alabama.................	996,992	987,030	9,962
Arkansas................	484,471	479,445	5,026
California..............	560,247	350,416	209,831
Connecticut...........	537,454	423,815	113,639
Delaware................	125,015	115,879	9,136
Florida....................	187,748	182,781	4,967
Georgia..................	1,184,109	1,172,982	11,127
Illinois.....................	2,539,891	2,024,693	515,198
Indiana..................	1,680,637	1,539,163	141,474
Iowa........................	1,194,020	989,328	204,692
Kansas....................	364,399	316,007	48,392
Kentucky...............	1,321,011	1,257,613	63,398
Louisiana................	726,915	665,088	61,827
Maine......................	626,915	578,034	48,881
Maryland...............	780,894	697,482	83,412
Massachusetts........	1,457,351	1,104,032	353,319
Michigan.................	1,184,059	916,049	268,010
Minnesota..............	439,706	279,009	160,697
Mississippi.............	827,922	816,731	11,191
Missouri.................	1,721,295	1,499,028	222,267

Nebraska	122,993	92,245	30,748
Nevada	42,491	23,690	18,801
New Hampshire	318,300	288,689	29,611
New Jersey	906,096	717,153	188,943
New York	4,382,759	3,244,406	1,138,353
North Carolina	1,071,361	1,068,332	3,029
Ohio	2,665,260	2,292,767	372,493
Oregon	90,923	79,323	11,600
Pennslyvania	3,521,951	2, 976,642	545,309
Rhode Island	217,353	161,957	55,396
South Carolina	705,606	697,532	8,074
Tennessee	1,258,520	1,239,204	19,316
Texas	818,579	756,168	62,411
Vermont	330,551	283,396	47,155
Virginia	1,225,163	1,211,409	13,754
West Virginia	442,014	424,923	17,091
Wisconsin	1,054,670	690,171	364,499
Total Territories	442,730	348,530	94,200
Arizona	9,658	3,849	5,809
Colorado	39,864	33,265	6,599
Dakota	14,181	9,366	4,815
Dist. of Columbia	131,700	??15,446	16,254
Idaho	14,999	7,114	7,885
Montana	20,595	12,616	7,979
New-Mexico	91,874	86,254	5,620
Utah	86,786	56,084	30,702
Washington	23,955	18,931	5,024
Wyoming	9,118	5,605	3,513

CITY POPULATION

POPULATION OF THE CITIES OF THE UNITED STATES
This table has been carefully compiled from the census (official copy) of 1870. It embraces all the cities returned as such, with a few that appear to have been omitted as cities distinctively.

States and Cities.	Total Population.
Alabama.	
Eufaula..................	3,185
Huntsville..............	4,907
Mobile.....................	32,034
Montgomery..........	10,588
Selma.....................	6,484
Talladega...............	1,933
Tuscaloosa.............	1,689
Tuscumbia.............	1,214
Total	62,034
Arkansas.	
Little Rock.............	12,380
California.	
Los Angeles...........	5,728
Marysville..............	4,738
Oakland.................	10,500
Sacramento...........	16,283
San Diego..............	2,300
San Francisco........	149,473
San Jose.................	9,089
Stockton................	10,066
Total	208,177

States and Cities.	Total Population.
Connecticut.	
Bridgeport.............	18,969
Hartford................	37,180
Middletown...........	6,923
New Haven............	50,840
Norwich.................	16,653
Waterbury.............	10,826
Total	141,391
Colorado.	
Denver...................	4,759
Delaware.	
Wilmington............	30,841
Dist. of Columbia.	
Georgetown...........	11,384
Washington...........	109,199
Total	120,583
Florida.	
Jacksonville...........	6,912
Pensecola...............	3,347
St. Augustine........	1,717
Tallahassee............	2,023
Total	13,999

States and Cities.	Total Population.	States and Cities.	Total Population.
Georgia.		Dixon	4,055
Athens	4,251	Elgin	5,441
Atlanta	21,789	El Paso	1,564
Augusta	15,389	Freeport	7,889
Columbus	7,401	Galena	7,019
Macon	10,810	Galesburg	10,158
Milledgeville	2,750	Jacksonville	9,203
Rome	2,748	Joliet	7,263
Savannah	28,235	La Salle	5,200
Total	93,373	Litchfield	3,852
Idaho.		Macomb	2,748
Boise City	995	Mendota	3,546
Idaho City	889	Monmouth	4,662
Silver City	599	Morris	3,138
Total	2,483	Mound City	1,631
Illinois.		Mt. Carmel	1,640
Alton	8,661	Olney	2,680
Amboy	2,825	Ottawa	7,736
Anna	1,269	Pekin	5,696
Aurora	11,162	Peoria	2,849
Belleville	8,146	Peru	3,650
Bloomington	14,590	Quincy	24,052
Bushnell	2,003	Rockford	11,049
Cairo	6,267	Rock Island	7,890
Canton	3,308	Shelbyville	2,051
Centralia	3,190	Springfield	17,364
Champaign	4,625	Sterling	3,998
Chicago	298,977	Watseca	1,551
Danville	4,751	Waukegan	4,507
Decatur	7,161	Total	571,021

States and Cities.	Total Population.	States and Cities.	Total Population.
Indiana.		Burlington	14,930
Columbia	1,663	Cedar Falls	3,070
Connorsville	2,496	Cedar Rapids	5,940
Crawfordsville	3,701	Clinton	6,129
Evansville	21,830	Council Bluffs	10,020
Fort Wayne	17,718	Davenport	20,038
Franklin City	2,707	Des Moines	12,035
Goshen	3,133	Dubuque	18,434
Greencastle	3,227	Fairfield	2,226
Indianapolis	48,244	Fort Dodge	3,095
Jeffersonville	7,254	Fort Madison	4,011
Kendallville	8,164	Glenwood	1,291
Lafayette	13,506	Independence	2,945
Laporte	6,581	Iowa City	5,314
Lawrenceburg	3,139	Keokuk	12,766
Logansport	8,950	Lyons	4,088
Madison	10,709	Maquoketa	1,756
Michigan City	3,985	Marshalltown	3,218
New Albany	15,396	McGregor	2,074
Peru	3,617	Muscatine	6,718
Richmond	9,445	Oskaloosa	3,204
Seymour	2,372	Ottawa	5,214
Shelbyville	2,731	Sioux City	3,401
South-Bend	7,206	Waterloo	4,337
Terre Haute	16,103	Waverley	2,291
Valparaiso	2,765	Winterset	1,485
Vincennes	5,440	Total	160,630
Wabash City	2,881	*Kansas.*	
Total	228,983	Atchison	7,054
Iowa.		Baxter Springs	1,284

States and Cities.	Total Population.	States and Cities.	Total Population.
Emporia	2,168	Augusta	7,808
Fort Scott	4,147	Bangor	18,289
Lawrence	8,320	Bath	7,371
Leavenworth	17,873	Belfast	5,278
Ottawa	2,941	Biddeford	10,282
Paola	1,811	Calais	5,944
Topeka	5,790	Hallowell	3,007
Wyandotte	2,940	Lewiston	13,600
Total	54,355	Portland	31,413
Kentucky.		Rockland	7,074
Covington	24,509	Total	116,235
Frankfort	5,336	*Maryland.*	
Henderson	4,171	Annapolis	5,744
Hopkinsville	3,136	Baltimore	267,354
Lexington	14,801	Frederick	8,526
Louisville	100,753	Hagerstown	5,779
Maysville	4,705	Total	287,403
Newport	15,087	*Massachusetts.*	
Owensboro	3,437	Boston	250,526
Paducah	6,866	Cambridge	39,634
Paris	2,655	Charlestown	28,323
Total	185,512	Chelsea	18,547
Louisiana.		Fall River	26,766
Baton Rouge	6,498	Haverhill	13,092
Donaldsonville	1,573	Lawrence	28,921
New Orleans	191,418	Lowell	40,928
Shreveport	4,607	Lynn	28,233
Total	204,096	New Bedford	21,320
Maine.		Newburypor	12,595
Auburn	6,169	Salem	24,117

States and Cities.	Total Population.	States and Cities.	Total Population.
Springfield.............	26,703	Saginaw.................	7,460
Taunton.................	18,629	St. Clair.................	1,790
Worcester...............	41,105	Wyandotte.............	2,731
Total	619,439	Ypsilanti................	5,471
Michigan.		Total	229,336
Adrian....................	8,438	*Minnesota.*	
Ann Arbor.............	7,363	Duluth....................	3,131
Battle Creek..........	5,838	Hastings.................	3,458
Bay City.................	7,064	Maukato................	3,482
Big Rapids.............	1,227	Minneapolis...........	13,066
Cold water.............	4,381	Owatonna.............	2,070
Corunna.................	?408	Red Wing...............	4,260
Detroit...................	79,577	Rochester...............	3,953
East Saginaw........	11,350	St. Anthony...........	5,013
Flint.......................	5,386	St. Cloud...............	2,161
Grand Haven........	3,147	St. Paul..................	20,030
Grand Rapids........	16,507	Winona...................	7,192
Hillsdale................	3,518	Total	67,816
Holland..................	2,319	*Mississippi.*	
Jackson..................	11,447	Columbus..............	4,812
Lansing..................	5,241	Grenada.................	1,887
Lapeer....................	1,772	Holly Springs........	2,406
Manistee................	3,343	Jackson..................	4,234
Marshall................	4,925	Macon....................	975
Monroe..................	5,986	Natchez.................	9,057
Muskegon..............	6,002	Vicksburgh.............	12,443
Miles......................	4,630	Total	35,814
Owasso...................	2,065	*Missouri.*	
Pontiac...................	4,867	Cape Girardeau.....	3,585
Port Huron............	5,973	Chillicothe.............	3,978

States and Cities.	Total Population.	States and Cities.	Total Population.
Hannibal	10,125	Atlantic City	1,043
Independence	3,184	Brighton	6,830
Jefferson City	4,420	Burlington	5,817
Kansas City	32,260	Camden	20,045
Louisiana	3,639	Elizabeth	20,832
Macon	3,678	Harrison	4,129
St. Charles	5,570	Hoboken	20,297
St. Joseph	19,565	Jersey City	82,546
St. Louis	310,864	Millville	6,101
Westport	1,095	Newark	105,059
Total	401,963	New Brunswick	15,058
Montana.		Orange	9,348
Helena	3,842	Paterson	33,579
Nebraska		Plainfield	5,095
Omaha	16,083	Princeton	2,798
Nebraska City	6,050	Rahway	6,258
Total	22,133	Trenton	22,874
Nevada.		Total	367,709
Austin	1,324	*New Mexico.*	
Carson City	3,042	Santa Fe	4,765
Virginia	7,048	*New York.*	
Total	11,414	Albany	69,422
New Hampshire.		Auburn	17,225
Concord	12,241	Binghamton	12,692
Dover	9,294	Brooklyn	396,099
Manchester	23,536	Buffalo	117,714
Nashna	10,543	Cohoes	15,357
Portsmouth	9,211	Elmira	15,863
Total	64,825	Hudson	8,615
New Jersey.		Lockport	12,426

States and Cities.	Total Population.	States and Cities.	Total Population.
New burg	17,014	Galliopolis	3,711
New York	942,292	Hamilton	11,081
Ogdensburg	10,076	Ironton	5,686
Oswego	20,910	Lancaster	4,725
Pough keepsie	20,080	Mansfield	8,029
Rochester	62,386	Marietta	5,218
Rome	11,000	Massillon	5,185
Schenectady	11,026	Mt. Vernon	4,876
Syracuse	43,051	Newark	6,698
Troy	46,465	Piqua	5,927
Utica	28,804	Pomeroy	5,824
Watertown	9,336	Portsmouth	10,592
Total	1,887,853	Sandusky	13,000
North Carolina.		Springfield	12,652
Charlotte	4,473	Steuben ville	8,107
Fayetteville	4,660	Tiffin	5,648
Newberne	5,849	Toledo	31,584
Raleigh	7,790	Urbana	4,276
Wilmington	13,446	Warren	3,457
Total	36,218	Wooster	5,419
Ohio.		Xenia	6,377
Akron	10,006	Youngstown	8,075
Canton	8,66?	Zanesville	10,011
Chillicothe	8,920	Total	595,461
Cincinnati	216,239	*Oregon.*	
Circleville	5,407	Oregon City	1,382
Cleveland	92,829	Portland	8,293
Columbus	31,274	Total	9,675
Dayton	30,473	*Pennsylvania.*	
Fremont	5,455	Allegheny	53,180

States and Cities.	Total Population.
Allentown	13,884
Altoona	10,610
Carbon dale	6,393
Chester	9,485
Columbia	6,461
Corry	6,809
Erie	19,646
Harrisburg	23,103
Lancaster	20,233
Lock Haven	6,989
Meadville	7,103
Philadelphia	674,022
Pittsburgh	86,076
Reading	33,930
Scranton	35,092
Titusville	8,639
Williamsport	16,030
York	11,003
Total	1,048,686
Rhode Island.	
Newport	12,521
Providence	68,964
Total	81,425
South Carolina.	
Charleston	48,956
Columbia	9,298
Total	58,254
Tennessee.	
Chattanooga	6,093
Knoxville	8,682

States and Cities.	Total Population.
Memphis	40,226
Nashville	25,865
Total	80,866
Texas.	
Austin	4,428
Brownsville	4,905
Galveston	13,818
Houston	9,382
San Antonio	12,256
Total	44,789
Utah.	
Logan	1,757
Manti	1,239
Mt. Pleasant	1,346
Ogden	3,127
Salt Lake City	12,854
Total	20,323
Vermont.	
Bennington	2,501
Brattleboro	4,933
Burlington	14,387
Middlebury	3,086
Montpelier	3,023
Rutland	9,834
St. Albans	7,014
St. Johnsbury	4,665
Total	49,443
Virginia.	
Alexandria	13,570
Fredericksb'gh	4,046

States and Cities.	Total Population.
Lynchburgh	6,825
Norfolk	19,229
Petersburgh	18,950
Portsmouth	10,492
Richmond	51,038
Total	124,150
West Virginia.	
Parkersburg	5,546
Wheeling	19,280
Total	24,826
Wisconsin.	
Appleton	4,518
Beaver Dam	3,265
Beloit	4,396

States and Cities.	Total Population.
Fond du Lao	12,764
Green Bay	4,666
Janesville	8,789
Kenosha	4,309
La Crosse	7,785
Madison	9,176
Manitowoc	5,168
Milwaukee	71,440
Oshkosh	12,663
Portage	3,945
Racine	9,880
Sheboygan	5,310
Watertown	7,550
Total	175,624

ORDER OF STATES IN POPULATION SIZE

ORDER OF THE STATES IN POINT OF POPULATION, AT SEVERAL PERIODS

	1790.	1830.	1850.	1870.
1	Virginia...............	New York............	New York............	New York.............
2	Massachusetts....	Pennsylvania......	Pennsylvania......	Pennsylvania.......
3	Pennsylvania......	Virginia...............	Ohio......................	Ohio......................
4	North Carolina...	Ohio......................	Virginia...............	Illinois..................
5	New York............	North Carolina...	Tennessee...........	Missouri...............
6	Maryland.............	Kentucky.............	Massachusetts....	Indiana.................
7	South Carolina...	Tennessee...........	Indiana................	Massachusetts.....
8	Connecticut........	Massachusetts....	Kentucky.............	Kentucky.............
9	New Jersey.........	South Carolina...	Georgia................	Tennessee............
10	New Hampshire.	Georgia................	North Carolina...	Virginia...............
11	Vermont..............	Maryland.............	Illinois..................	Iowa.....................
12	Georgia................	Maine...................	Alabama..............	Georgia................
13	Kentucky.............	Indiana................	Missouri..............	Michigan.............
14	Rhode Island.......	New Jersey.........	South Carolina...	North Carolina....
15	Delaware.............	Alabama..............	Mississippi..........	Wisconsin............
16	Tennessee...........	Connecticut........	Maine...................	Alabama...............
17		Vermont..............	Maryland.............	New Jersey..........
18		New Hampshire.	Louisiana............	Mississippi...........
19		Louisiana............	New Jersey.........	Texas....................
20		Illinois..................	Michigan.............	Maryland.............
21		Missouri..............	Connecticut........	Louisiana.............
22		Mississippi..........	New Hampshire.	South Carolina....
23		Rhode Island.......	Vermont..............	Maine....................
24		Delaware.............	Wisconsin............	California.............
25		Florida.................	Texas....................	Connecticut..........
26		Michigan.............	Arkansas..............	Arkansas..............
27		Arkansas.............	Iowa.....................	West Virginia.......

28			Rhode Island........	Kansas....................
29			California.............	Minnesota............
30			Delaware.............	Vermont...............
31			Florida.................	New Hampshire..
32			Minnesota...........	Rhode Island........
33				Florida..................
34				Delaware..............
35				Nebraska..............
36				Oregon.................
37				Nevada.................

Order of territories, 1870

District of Columbia, New Mexico, Utah, Washington, Montana, Idaho, Dacotah, Arizona, Wyoming. The census of Alaska has not been taken.

STATE BY RACE

POPULATION OF STATES BY RACES

	Whites.	Colored.	Indians.
Alabama............................	521,384	475,510	98
Arizona.............................	9,581	26	31
Arkansas...........................	362,115	122,169	89
*California........................	499,424	4,272	7,241
Colorado............................	39,221	456	180
Connecticut.......................	527,449	9,668	239
Dakota..............................	12,887	94	1,200
Delaware...........................	102,221	22,794	
District of Columbia........	88,278	43,404	15
Florida..............................	96,057	91,689	2
Georgia.............................	638,926	545,142	4
Idaho................................	10,618	60	47
Illinois..............................	2,511,096	28,762	32

57

Indiana	1,655,837	24,560	240
Iowa	1,188,207	5,762	48
Kansas	346,377	17,108	914
Kentucky	1,098,692	222,210	108
Louisiana	362,065	364,210	569
Maine	624,809	1,606	499
Maryland	605,497	175,391	4
*Massachusetts	1,443,156	13,947	151
Michigan	1,167,282	11,849	4,926
Minnesota	438,257	759	690
Mississippi	382 896	444,201	809
Missouri	1,603,146	118,071	75
Montana	18,306	183	157
Kebraska	122,117	789	87
Nevada	38,959	357	23
New Hampshire	317,697	580	23
*New Jersey	875,407	30,658	16
New Mexico	90,393	172	1,309
New York	4,330,210	52,081	439
North Carolina	678,470	391,650	1,241
Ohio	2,601,946	63,213	100
Oregon	86,929	346	318
Pennsylvania	3,456,609	65,294	34
Rhode Island	212,219	4,980	154
South Carolina	289,667	415,814	124
Tennessee	936,119	322,331	70
Texas	564,700	253,475	379
Utah	86,044	118	175
Vermont	329,613	924	14
Virginia	712,089	512,841	229
Washington Territory	22,195	207	1,319
West Virginia	424,033	17,980	1
Wisconsin	1,051,351	2,113	1,206
Wyoming	8,726	183	66

* Japanese :—California, 33; Massachusetts, 10; New Jersey 10.

AREA OF UNITED STATES

AREA OF THE UNITED STATES.	*Acres.*
Total area of the Public Lands of the States and Territories	1,792,844,160
Total area of those States where there are no Public Lands	476,546,560
Area of Indian Territory	44,154,240
Area of District of Columbia	38,400
Grand total of area of the United States, in acres	2,311,583,360 or, Three Million Six Hundred Eleven Thousand Eight Hundred and Forty nine square Miles.

This docs not include the area of the great Lakes just within and forming a portion of our Northern boundary; neither does it include the marine league on the coast.

INDIVIDUAL STATES OF THE UNION

HISTORICAL AND STATISTICAL TABLE OF THE UNITED STATES OF NORTH AMERICA

[*Note.*—The whole area of the United States, including water surface of lakes and rivers, is nearly equal to four million square miles, embracing the Russian purchase.]

The Thirteen Original States.	SETTL'D	Sq. miles	*Pop. 1870.
New Hampshire	1623	9,280	318,300
Massachusetts	1620	7,800	1,457,351
Rhode Island	1636	1,306	217,353
Connecticut	1633	4,750	537,454
New York	1613	47,000	4,382,759
New Jersey	1624	8,320	906,096
Pennsylvania	1681	46,000	3,521,791
Delaware	1627	2,120	125,015
Maryland	1634	11,124	780,894
Virginia—East and West	1607	61,352	1,667,177
North Carolina	1650	50,704	1,071,361
South Carolina	1670	34,000	705,606
Georgia	1733	58,000	1,184,109

* The total population of the United States in 1860 was, in round numbers, 31,500,000. In 1865 it is estimated that the population was 35,500,000, including the inhabitants of the Territories, estimated at 360,000 persons on January 1,1865. The Census of 1870 made the whole number about 39,000,000 ; at the end of the present century it will be, probably, 103,000,000.

THE STATES ADMITTED INTO THE UNION

states admitted.	Settled.	act admitting state.	area in sq. miles.	population, 1870.
Kentucky...............	1774	Feb. 4, 1791	37,680	1,323,264
Vermont.................	1724	Feb. 18, 1791	10,212	330,558
Tennessee..............	1756	June 1, 1796	45,600	1,258,326
Ohio.......................	1788	April 30, 1802	39,964	2,675,468
Lousiana................	1699	April 8, 1812	41,346	734,420
Indiana..................	1730	Dec. 11, 1816	33,809	1,668,169
Mississippi.............	1540	Dec. 10, 1817	47,156	842,056
Illinois....................	1683	Dec. 3, 1818	55,410	2,567,036
Alabama................	1713	Dec. 14, 1819	50,722	996,175
Maine....................	1623	March 3, 1820	35,000	630,423
Missouri................	1763	March 2, 1821	65,350	1,725,658
Arkansas...............	1685	June 15, 1836	52,198	486,103
Michigan...............	1670	Jan. 26, 1837	56,451	1,184,653
Florida...................	1565	March 3, 1845	59,268	189,950
Iowa.......................	1778	March 3, 1845	55,045	1,181,359
Texas.....................	1694	Dec. 29, 1845	274,356	795,590
Wisconsin..............	1669	March 3, 1847	53,924	1,055,501
California..............	1769	Sept. 9, 1850	188,981	556,208
Minnesota..............	1654	Feb. 26, 1857	83,531	424,543
Oregon...................	1792	Feb, 14, 1859	95,274	90,878
Kansas...................	1849	Jan. 29, 1861	81,318	379,497
West Virginia.........	1607	Dec. 31, 1862	23,000	447,943
Nevada...................	1848	Mar. 21, 1864	112,090	44,686
Colorado...............	....	....	104,500	39,681
Nebraska...............	1852	March 1, 1867	75,995	116,888

TERRITORIES.	WHEN SETTLED.	AREA IN SQ. MILES.	POPULATION, 1870.
Wyoming.............................	1866	97,883	9,118
New Mexico.........................	1570	121,201	92,604
Utah.....................................	1847	84,746	70,000
Washington.........................	1840	69,994	23,925
Dakota.................................	1850	150,932	14,181
Arizona................................	1600	113,916	9,658
Idaho...................................	1862	86,294	14,882
Montana..............................	1862	143,776	20,594
India....................................	1832	68,991	....
District of Columbia..........	1771	10 miles sq.	131,706
North-western America, purchased by treaty of May 28, 1867......................	1799	557,390	67,000

POLICE STATISTICS IN VARIOUS CITIES

New York – Number of officers 2,600; Patrolmen's pay $100 per month; Sergeants' pay $138 per month; Captains' $166 per month; latest census, 1875, 1,046,037; number of arrests 78,451; average per officer 37; square miles 41; Superintendent, G. W. Walling.

Philadelphia – Number of Patrolmen 1,200; 1876, arrests 44,919; Patrolmen's pay $2.25 per diem; Captains' pay $125 per month: Sergeants pay $90.20 per month; Population 1876, 817,488; K. H. Jones, Chief of Police. Square miles 12538/100; square acres 82,803; Park Police 114; number of Buildings Jan. 1st, 1876, 145,001; 4 Captains; 26 Lieutenants; 62 Sergeants.

Brooklyn – Number of officers 567; Patrolmen's pay $100 per month; Sergeants' pay $133 per month; Captains' $166 per month; official census, 1870, 396,099; number of arrests 25,558; average per officer 45; square miles 25; Superintendent, Patrick Campbell.

St. Louis – Number of officers 439; Patrolmen's pay $75 per month; Sergeants' pay $100 per month; Captains' $150 per month; official census, 1870, 310,864; number of arrests 19,082; average per officer 51; square miles 5.2; Superintendent, James McDonough.

Boston – Number of officers 630; Patrolmen's pay $90 per month; Sergeants' pay $100 per month; Captains' pay $150 per month; official census, 1870, 250,526; number of arrests 25,261; average per officer 51; square miles 104; Superintendent, Wm. Savage.

Baltimore – Number of officers 592; Patrolmen's pay $78 per month; Sergeants' pay $82 per month; Lieutenants' pay $86 per month; Captains' pay $92 per month; official census, 1870, 267,354; number of arrests 26,365; average per officer 47; square miles 16; Superintendent, John T. Gray.

New Orleans – Number of officers 585; official census, 1870, 191,418; number of arrests 21,286; average per officer 50; square miles 150, Superintendent, W. F. Loan.

Chicago – Number of officers 507; Patrolmen's pay $850 per year; Sergeants' pay $1,220 per year; Chief's pay $1,615 per year; population 298,977; square miles 40; Superintendent, M. C. Hickey.

Cincinnati – Number of officers 332; Patrolmen's pay $66.67; Lieutenants' pay $75 per month; official census, 1870, 216,239; number of arrests 4,517; average per officer 26; square miles 24; Superintendent, Ira Wood.

Columbus, O. – Number of officers 37; number of arrests 4,031; average per officer 109; Superintendent, Samuel Thompson.

Buffalo – Number of officers 203; Patrolmen's pay $66.67 per month; Sergeants' pay $75 per month; Captains', $100 per month; official census, 1870, 118,000; number of arrests 8,858; average per officer 44; square miles 27; Superintendent, John Byrnes.

Albany – Number of officers 112; Patrolmen's pay $68 per month; Lieutenants' pay $85 per month; Captains' pay $116 per month; official census, 1870, 69,422; number of arrests 6,373; average per officer 56; square miles 22; Superintendent, John Maloy.

San Francisco – Number of officers 150; Patrolmen's pay $125 gold, per month; Sergeants' pay $150 per month; Captains', $175 per month; official census, 1870, 149,473; number of arrests 20,108; average per officer 134; square miles 37. 5; Superintendent, H. H. Ellis.

Washington – Number of officers 232; Patrolmen's pay $90 per month; Sergeants' pay $100 per month; Lieutenants' pay $150 per month; official census, 1870, 109,099; number of arrests 14,226; average per officer 62; square miles 14; Superintendent, A. C. Richards.

Cleveland – Number of officers 171; Patrolmen's pay $825 per year; Sergeants' pay $930 per year; Lieutenants' pay $1,020 per year; Captains' pay 1,400 per year; official census, 1870, 92,229; square miles 29; Superintendent, J. W. Schmitt.

Toledo – Number of officers 52; Patrolmen's pay $720 per year; Sergeants' pay $800 per year; Chief's pay $1,700 per year: official census, 1870, 31,584; square miles 16; Superintendent, J. C. Purdy.

Milwaukie – Number of officers 62; Patrolmen's pay $66 per month; Sergeants' pay $75 per month; Captains'pay $80 per month; official census, 1870, 71,440; square miles 13; Superintendent, Wm. Beck.

Worcester – Number of officers 50; Patrolmen's pay $820 per year; Captains' pay $900 per year; Chiefs pay $1,600 per year; population 41,405; square miles 12; Superintendent, Ansel Washburne.

Chelsea, Mass – Number of officers 22; Patrolmen's pay $2.25 per day; Sergeants' pay $2.50 per day; Captains'pay $3 per day; official census, 1870, 18,547; square miles 1. 8; Superintendent, Wm. P. Drury.

Jersey City – Number of force 165; Four stations 2 subs.; Chief Benjamin Murphy, salary $2,000; Four Captains $1,500; Sixteen Sergeants $960; Patrolmen $840. The numerical strength of Department is considered inadequate in proportion to number of population, valuation of property and area square miles to patrol.

Charleston, S. C. – Number of officers 138; official census, 1870, 48,956; number of arrests 2,705; average per officer 20; square miles 16; Superintendent, H. W. Hendricks.

Newark, N. J. – Number of officers 177; official census, 1870, 105,059; number of arrests 6,752; average per officer 38; Superintendent, Jno. Mills.

Salem, Mass. – Number of officers 42; official census, 1870, 24,117; number of arrests 1,682; average per officer 40; Superintendent, —Hill.

Indianapolis, Ind. – Number of officers 62; Patrolmen's pay $900 per year; Captains' pay $1,200 per year; official census, 1870, 48,244; Superintendem, A. C. Dewey.

Covington, Ky. – Number of officers 20; Patrolmen's pay $720 per year; Lieutenant's pay $1,200 per year; official census, 1870, 24,502; Superintendent, P. J. Bolan.

Lowell – Number of officers 52; Patrolmen's pay $900 per year; Captains' pay $1,200, Chief's pay $1,800 per year; population 40,928

Alleghany – Number of officers 57; Patrolmens' pay $803 per year; Captains' pay $900 per year; Chief's pay $1,000 per year; population 53,180; number of arrests 2,641.

Oswego – Number of officers 11; Patrolmen's pay $60 per month; Captains' pay $960 per year; population 20,910; number of arrests 1,117; Chief, Nathan Lee.

Providence – Number of officers 191; Patrolmens' pay $1,080 per year; Captains' pay $1,300 per year; Chief's pay $1,250; number of arrests 8,964.

Richmond – Number of officers 84; Patrolmens' pay $900 per year; Captains' pay $1,200 per year; Chief's pay $2,000 per year; population 51,038; number of arrests 6,800.

Utica – Number of officers 20; Patrolmens' pay $720 per year; Assistant Chief's pay $960 per year; Chief's pay $1,200 per year; population 28,804; number of arrests, 1876, 1,200; average per officer 60; square miles 8; cost Dept. $16,000; Chief, James Dwyer.

Syracuse – Number of officers 34; Patrolmen's pay $75 per month; Captains' pay $1,200 per year; Chief's pay $1,500 per year; population 60,000; number of arrests, 1876, 3,360; arerage per officer 33; Chief, Thomas Davis.

Norfolk – Population, 1870, 19,256; number of force 44; Chief's pay $3 per day; Assistant Chief's pay $2.75 per day; Patrolmen's pay $2 per day; 18 hours' duty in 48; number of arrests, 1876, 1,977.

Reading – Number of officers 28; pay $45 per month with uniform; Chief's pay $950 per year; population 33,000; Chief, Peter Cullin.

Harrisburg – Population 30,000; Chief, Christian Cilley; pay $900 per year; Lieutenant's pay $780 per year; Officers' pay $600 per year; square miles 3½.

Scranton – Population 35,000; Chief, Jack Breese; number of officers 11; pay $75 per month.

Dayton – Population, 1870, 30,473; number of force 35; Chief's pay $1,440 per year; Sergeants' pay $900 per year; Boundsmen's pay $850 per year; Patrolmen's pay $800 per year; 11 hours' duty every 24; Chief, Amos Clark.

London, Eng. – Number of officers 8,833; population in 1878, 3,533,184; number of arrests 42,951; average per officer 8; square miles 122; Superintendent, J. T. Willmayer.

Liverpool, Eng. – Number of officers 1,018; population in 1878, 527,000; number of arrests 32,243; average per officer 32; square miles 12; Superintendent, Anthony Jones.

Manchester, Eng. – Number of officers 682; population in 1878, 400,000; number of arrests 31,158; average per officer 46; Superintendent, W. H. Palin, Ch. Con.

Dublin, Ireland – Number of officers 2,085; population in 1878, 314,666; number of arrests 32,243; average per officer 16; square miles 5.

IMMIGRATION

A survey of Immigration to the USA from 1783 to 1878

By an Act of Congress approved March 2, 1818, Collectors of Customs were required to keep a record, and make a quarterly return to the Treasury of all passengers arriving in their respective districts from Foreign Ports and these reports, duly condensed in the Department, are the chief bases of our knowledge of the subsequent growth and progress of Immigration.

IMMIGRATION, FROM 1783 to 1878

Of the Immigrants who landed on our shores in the *fifty-eight years* ending with June 30, 1878 (1820 to 1878) there came from different countries as follows:

Great Britain and Ireland..	4,547,331	Belgium............................	21,667
France..................................	301,277	Denmark..........................	43 079
West Indies...........................	75,149	Portugal...........................	7,173
Sweden and Norway	301,211	Turkey..............................	552
S. America............................	9,128	Greece..............................	338
Africa....................................	828	Austro Hungary.............	80,614
Spain.....................................	25,922	Japan................................	351
Russia and Poland...............	47,286	Asia, not specified..........	519
Switzerland...........................	78,707	British North America...	470,525
China....................................	196,252	Central Amer..................	1,414
Germany...............................	2,910,026	Australia, &c...................	18,529
Holland.................................	42,455	Countries not specified..	312,363
Mexico..................................	23,585	Total 58 years	9,576,569
Italy......................................	60,228		

Of the 3,734,248 passengers landed at Castle Garden from August 1, 1855, to January 1, 1879, their avowed destinations were as follows:

New York and Undecided	1,501,531	N. Carolina	1,015
Maine	6,164	S. Carolina	3,567
New Hampsh'r	4,120	Georgia	3,020
Vermont	6,210	Florida	710
Massachusetts	170,024	Alabama	1,452
Rhode Island	34,273	Mississippi	1,405
Connecticut	67,800	Louisiana	6,568
New Jersey	115,566	Texas	3,329
Pennsylvania	381,614	Arkansas	626
Delaware	3,404	Tennessee	6,432
Maryland	27,103	Kentucky	16,436
Dis. Columbia	11,297	Ohio	191,434
Virginia	10,427	Michigan	92,717
W. Virginia	1,636	Indiana	46,848
		Illinois	345,894

Wisconsin............	175,199	Canada.................	69,765
Iowa.....................	81,598	N. Brunsw'k........	12,205
Missouri...............	67,780	Nova Scotia.........	145
Minnesota...........	66,389	New Foundl'd......	2
Kansas.................	19,503	New D minion.....	816
Nebraska.............	18,950	S. America...........	770
Dakota.................	4,729	Cuba.....................	404
Colorado..............	2,284	Lima.....................	24
Wyoming..............	271	Mexico.................	389
Utah.....................	35,390	Bermudas and other W. In...........	255
Montana..............	322		
Idaho....................	195	Central Am..........	116
Nevada.................	1,725	N. W. Coast..........	473
Arizona................	3	Australia..............	52
New Mexico.........	2,179	Sandwich Isl's.....	7
California............	48,210	Japan....................	10
Oregon and Wash. Ter............	844	China....................	21
		Vancouver's I......	1
Other Countries.		Unknown.............	22,036
Brit. Colum.........	88		

The total arrivals of Immigrants into the United States in the year ending June 30, 1878, was 138,469; of whom 38,082 were from the United Kingdom of Great Britain and Ireland; 29,313; from Germany; 33,437 from other European Countries; 25,571 from British America; 8,994 from China and Japan; 672 from the Azores; 1,019 from the West Indies; 11 from the East Indies; 88 from South America, and the remainder from other countries.

LABOR

THE LABOR QUESTION

In a work like this – devoted to the highest interests of the workingmen of all classes, whether their labor is mechanical, agricultural, commercial, manufacturing or intellectual – questions pertaining to the employment of labor, the hours of working, and the average remuneration of different classes of workingmen should be fairly considered.

There is a prevalent disposition among workingmen to regard the employer and employed as classes hostile to each other, and as having interests which are diametrically opposed to each other. This we believe to be not only a very narrow, but an entirely false view. Were it true, there would be no work done in civilized countries, except what every man could do for himself. A man wants a house built; he must build it for himself, on this theory, though there might be a hundred workmen who desire to labor on it; for, the moment he seeks to employ others to do this work, he becomes an employer, a capitalist, and his position is hostile to that of the men he employs. He can have no object in life, but to use his money to oppress and distress them; while they, in return, look upon him with envy and hatred, because he is their natural antagonist and oppressor. The theory

once stated in this plain way, even the most ignorant can see its fallacy.

What we have to say in regard to the labor question here, concerns only labor in the United States. We have nothing to do with the labor question in Russia, Germany, France, Italy or Great Britain. The government of those countries, and the conditions under which alone labor is possible there, are entirely different from ours. Here, So long as he violates no law, and does no injustice to his fellow man, the workingman possesses the same rights and privileges as the capitalist. For him to resort to violence, and oppose the government which he himself has had a hand in making, is as absurd as it was for the petted child who when his wearied mother said "Well, let him have what he wants," to exclaim, "I won't have what I want."

If the workingman has not all his just rights under our government, it is his fault. He is one of the law makers; let him ask for these just laws and he will get them.

A word, then, about the title, "Capitalist." What is a Capitalist in this country? He is, in most cases, a man who, beginning as a workingman has, by industry, economy and good management, saved his earnings to such an extent as to be able to employ others. His income being thus increased, extends his business till he employs hundreds and perhaps thousands of his late fellow workmen. Is it supposable that such a man will forget that he himself has been a workingman, or that he will become hostile to the interests of those with whom he has wrought day after day? I suppose that the late Cornelius Vanderbilt was the largest Capitalist employing labor, in our time. Yet who that has read his history does not know that in early life he was not only a workingman, but one of the most laborious of workingmen? Asa Packer, the largest proprietor of Coal Mines in America, and the man who single handed, has been able to prevent the great Coal Companies from forming a combination which would prove disadvantageous to the public, was, at the age of 28, a day-laborer, earning but fifty or sixty cents a day. There are hundreds more whom we might name.

No one was compelled to work for them, if their rate of compensation was less than could be obtained for the same work elsewhere; and it is not, we believe, pretended that they paid, on the average, less wages than the others. So far, then, there is nothing to awaken hostility between employers and employed. It was not assumed that these men were perfect, or honest, upright, and benevolent in their business, beyond the average of men. They were men of like passions and dispositions with the rest of us.

But now, after a season of excessive commercial prosperity, and high prices, the result in part of an inflated currency, there comes a time of financial depression. If our capitalist is a manufacturer, he finds his goods will not sell, or if they are sold at all, it must be at a price below their actual cost, and consequently, in the long run, he must reduce the cost of manufacture, or become a bankrupt. Is it wrong, that he should say to his employees, I cannot afford to pay the highest prices, I must reduce your wages by such a percentage. If others will pay more, of course they have the right to go where they can receive the largest wage, but if a part of their number, or others, who are out of work, choose to accept his terms, which it is fair to presume are the best he can afford, those who leave his employ have no right to molest or obstruct those who choose to remain in it. If the capitalist has reduced his wages too low, below those paid by others in the same business or below what is a living rate, and all his employees leave him – and others as competent will not take their places – he soon finds out his mistake and is ready to compromise.

Much is said of the soullessness of corporations, and it is often asserted that the oppression of workingmen is more frequent where they are employed by corporations. We doubt this – a company which is honestly and ably managed, is governed by the same principles as an individual capitalist. It must manage its affairs economically or its stockholders will suffer loss; as a general rule, corporations pay higher wages, especially in prosperous times. Engaged in the same or similar lines of business, corporations and individual businessmen sometimes associate together, acting in concert in regard to the amount of production, wages and other matters appertaining to their united interests. Working men often take exception to these associations, and denounce them as hostile to the working classes.

We cannot see the reasonableness of this. As a general rule, these associations have proved beneficial to both employers and employed. A comparison of views has tended to shorten rather than protract the hours of labor, and to advance the amount of wages. It has also led to what workingmen should be thankful for, a classification and discrimination in regard to the skill and capacity of employees, by which higher wages have been paid to the industrious and skilled workman, while the indolent have either been dismissed, or remanded to low wages till their work was improved.

This much we have felt it right and just to say for the employers. Now let us consider the rights and privileges that the workingman and working woman may claim.

Let us begin negatively. No human being has an absolute right to compel another to employ him, be that other an individual capitalist, a corporation, or the state. Man has a right to live, if he can, by honest toil, of hand, of foot, or brain; but he has no right to compel an individual, a corporation or the state, to support him. He has no right to obtain his living by theft or violence. In a normal condition of society, there is enough work to employ every honest, intelligent, temperate and industrious man who has the health to work. But for the purpose of bringing the employers and employees together it is sometimes necessary that some must emigrate if they desire employment.

When business is depressed, the intemperate, the improvident, the ignorant, and the worthless are sure to be thrown out of employment. No Trades Union or organization can prevent it.

Hence the necessity, that workingmen and their children should be educated for their business, that they should be strictly temperate, honest and industrious. The employee who seeks to make the interest of his employer his own interest, and is watchful against any loss or injury to it, in ninety-nine cases out of a hundred, he will find that his faithfulness has been noticed, if it has not been commended, and that though others may be dismissed, he will be retained.

It is the undoubted right of every workingman to refuse to work for an employer, if his wages are reduced below what he regards as a just compensation. This is usually called "a strike," and whether it produces its intended effect or not, that of compelling the employers to raise the price of work, it is nonetheless the right and privilege of the workingman to refuse the work.

Trades Unions are not objectionable in themselves, on the contrary they often times are the means of doing great good to the members, and to their families. It is only when they are perverted from their true purpose that they become mischievous. In the early history of the Trades Unions in Great Britain they were hot-beds of crime. The workingmen goaded to revenge by the oppression which they suffered, resisted by arson, assassination and murder, all the attempts of the employers to employ non-union men, or to employ any greater or less number of men, or men of greater efficiency, or at any other wages than they prescribed. But these times and deeds have passed away, never again to return. Workingmen now understand better than they did formerly the natural laws which govern labor.

Trades Unions, as at present constituted, are mainly Mutual Benefit Associations, which by small weekly payments, usually of from 20 to 30 cents per week, provide a fund for the care of sick members, the burial of the dead, the providing for the widows and orphans, the aid of the infirm, disabled or unemployed, if temperate and of reputable character. They also negotiate with the employers, with whom they endeavor to maintain friendly relations, keep a general supervision over wages, recognizing the difference (which the old Trades Unions did not) between skilled and unskilled workmen, prevent strikes, when possible, by mediation, and where they prove inevitable, grant such assistance to the strikers in money or supplies as may be required. The best and strongest of these Unions avoid carefully any political action, and will not sell themselves to any party.

In Great Britain within the past twenty-five years these Unions have attained to great influence, the total number of members in England in 1878, being, it is said, about 1,500,000. Among their other work there they encourage emigration, and aid emigrant members to find a new home in Canada, Australia, Tasmania, New Zealand, and to some extent in the United States.

In general, Trades Unions of the better class have not been as successful in the United States as in Great Britain. There is some

reason to hope that they may become more so in the future. They have in many cases been only organizations of a single trade, as the Typographical Unions for the Printers, the St. Crispins for the Shoemakers, the Locomotive Engineers for that class, &c., and have, in many instances, come into violent and protracted collisions with the employers which have engendered a bitter hostility. Of late the inclination to consolidate several trades or callings in one society, has been gaining ground, and every such organization is to be encouraged, as it liberalizes and enlarges the field of the workingmen, and renders them more tolerant of the rights of employers, and less disposed to violence. The Workingmen's Central Union of Boston is one of the latest and most successful of these. In all, the future for British workingmen has a gloomy outlook, while in our own country we seem to be passing into an era of great prosperity.

The following table gives the wages actually paid in Massachusetts, on the gold standard, in 1878, being a year of great depression. The probabilities are that there, as well as elsewhere, wages will appreciate to a moderate degree with returning prosperity. We also give the average retail prices of Groceries, Provisions, Fuel, Dry Goods, Bents, &c., for the same years.

AVERAGE WEEKLY WAGE, 1878

Occupations.	Average Weekly Wage, Gold Stnd'rd 1878. $	Occupations.	Average Weekly Wage, Gold Stnd'rd 1878. $
Agriculture.		Wood-Workers....	11 50
Lab'rs per mo. & board..................	$15 72	Finishers.............	13 50
		Helpers................	8 83
Lab'rs pr day, no bo'rd..................	1 25	Laborers..............	6 75
		Blacksmiths........	13 75
Arms & Ammunition.		*Bleach'g,Dy'ng, Prn'tg*	
Machinist............	18 00	Overseers............	20 77
Machinists, foremen...............	37 50	Engine Tenders..	11 00
Inspectors...........	15 00	Printers..............	26 40
Inspectors, foremen...............	30 00	Back Tenders......	6 65
		Dyers...................	6 00
Fitters.................	16 50	Designers............	25 00
Tool-Maker.........	17 12	Engravers...........	23 80
Armorers.............	14 25	Driers..................	5 50
Watchmen...........	12 50	Starchers,...........	5 75
Firemen..............	13 50	Finishers and Packers................	7 07
Engineers............	15 00	Soapers................	6 00
Laborers..............	8 00	Dyers and Steamers.............	6 00
Boys.....................	6 00		
Artisans' Tools.		Singers.................	6 75
Pattern-Makers..	18 00	Engineers............	9 00
File-Cutters........	8 00	Carpenters..........	9 00
Machinists..........	12 75	Teamsters...........	8 40
Hardeners...........	8 00	Mechanics, repairs.................	13 50
Forgers................	15 00		
Moulders.............	14 40	Color-Mixers.......	6 12

Occupations.	Average Weekly Wage, Gold Stnd'rd 1878. $
Watchmen	8 90
Firemen	7 50
Men	6 33
Women	4 95
Boys	3 90
Girls	4 80
Boys and Girls	3 60
Laborers	6 37
Bookbinders.	
Gilders	20 00
Finishers	17 77
Forwarders	16 20
F'ldrs & Sewers, w'mn	6 05
Collators, women	6 32
Boots and Shoes.	
Cutters	11 05
Bottomers	10 71
Machine-Closers	14 25
Boot-Treers	12 00
Crimpers	10 00
Fitters	12 00
Finishers	11 75
Buffers	19 50
Edge-Setters	13 00
Shoemakers	8 00
Machine Hands, w'mn	7 33

Occupations.	Average Weekly Wage, Gold Stnd'rd 1878. $
McKay Operators	17 75
Beaters	8 00
Beaters-out	15 00
Trimmers	12 25
Women	8 00
Boxes.	
Men	11 57
Women and Girls	5 09
Boys	5 00
Bread, Crackers, Etc.	
Bread-Bakers	11 97
Cracker-Bakers	12 00
Drivers	16 61
Shippers	12 00
Packers, Women	7 87
Breweries.	
Teamsters	12 00
Engineers	14 75
Watchmen	9 66
Carpenters	12 00
Painters	12 00
Wash-House	10 96
Mash-Floor	12 81
Coopers	15 00
Bricks.	
Moulders	3 37
Sorters	3 12

Occupations.	Average Weekly Wage, Gold Stnd'rd 1878. $	Occupations.	Average Weekly Wage, Gold Stnd'rd 1878. $
Loaders	3 96	Boys	5 00
Barrow-men	3 85	*Building Trades.*	
Overseers	8 50	Carpenters	11 33
Engineers	7 50	Painters &	13 85
Carpenters	6 00	Glaziers	
Pressers	5 36	Steam & Gas	12 16
Face-Brick men	7 06	Fitters	
Burners'	13 57	Slaters	12 50
Assistants		Paper-Hangers	16 45
Laborers	3 00	Plumbers	18 00
Teamsters	3 77	Plasterers	12 25
Hostlers	3 00	Masons	13 37
Blacksmiths	4 00	Carpenters'	8 29
Brushes.		Laborers	
Finishers	13 48	Mas. & Plast.	8 13
Finishers, low gr'd w'k	6 00	Laborers	
		Cabinet Making.	
Nailers	17 10	Chair-Makers	$11 00
Paint-Brush Makers	18 00	Decorators	24 00
		Gilders	17 00
Do Fine Work	25 00	Turners	11 60
Painters	15 10	Carvers	12 33
Borers	15 10	Cabinet-Makers	11 03
Combers	14 24	Mill-Men	10 67
Combers, low gr'd w'k	8 00	Polishers & Finishers	10 25
Washers	8 00	Upholsterers	11 42
Pan-hands, women	5 01	Upholst. sewers, w'mn	7 00
Drawers, women	4 70	*Carpetings.*	

Occupations.	Average Weekly Wage, Gold Stnd'rd 1878. $	Occupations.	Average Weekly Wage, Gold Stnd'rd 1878. $
Wool-Sorters.......	9 25	Painters...............	14 56
Wool-Washers.....	7 25	Carriage-Part	14 14
Wool-Preparers..	6 50	Makers................	
Combers..............	6 30	Wheelwrights.....	13 70
Finishers.............	5 57	Trimmers...........	15 80
Dyers and	7 50	Blacksmiths........	15 24
Dryers.................		Blacksmiths'	9 00
Drawing in..........	7 13	Helpers...............	
Filling Boys........	3 50	*Corsets.*	
Drawers..............	6 50	Forewoman.........	7 66
Dressers..............	10 50	Overlookers........	5 71
Weavers..............	8 50	Embroiderers.....	6 47
Burlers................	4 70	Needle-Hands.....	5 37
Section Hands....	10 33	Finishers &	4 50
Drawers and	4 35	Packers................	
Spinners..............		Machine-Hands..	6 02
Doffers................	3 00	Boners.................	4 00
Frame-Spinners.	5 00	Eyeleters.............	6 37
Twisters..............	9 00	Binders...............	6 78
Carders..............	16 75	Cutters................	7 00
Firemen..............	7 00	Cutters, men.......	12 00
Packers................	7 50	Pressers..............	7 50
Overseers............	27 00	Pressers, men.....	14 00
Machn'sts &	11 00	Custom Work......	5 00
Carpnt'rs............		*Clothing–Ready-Made.*	
Watchmen...........	10 00	Overseers............	24 82
Laborers..............	7 05	Cutters................	16 00
Laborers' Boys...	3 75	Trimmers............	14 31
Carriages.		Pressers..............	10 28
Body-Makers......	15 70	Basters, women..	6 46

Occupations.	Average Weekly Wage, Gold Stnd'rd 1878. $	Occupations.	Average Weekly Wage, Gold Stnd'rd 1878. $
Mach'n-oper's, women	5 92	Second Hands	8 00
		Section Hands	11 40
Finsh'rs. at home, wmn	3 46	General Hands	6 44
		Young Persons	3 72
Finishers, shop, wm'n	4 58	Spare Hands	4 00
		Mule Spinners	7 41
Finishers, contr. wm'n	3 50	Mule Spinners, wm'n	4 00
Finishers, cust'm, wmn	8 00	Mule Spinners, boys	1 68
Pants, Vest, Cust. Wrk	6 90	Back-Boys	2 32
		Doffers	4 65
Cotton Goods.		Frame Spinners	3 96
Openers and Pickers	$6 23	Frame Sp'nrs, b's & g's	3 34
" Boys	3 45	Frame Spinners, girls	3 52
Strippers	5 06		
Strippers & Grinders	7 95	Frame Spinners, boys	2 70
Grinders	7 34	Frame Spinners, w'mn	2 83
Frame Tenders	4 47		
Drawers	3 70	Ring Spinners, overs'r	18 00
Railway & Alley Boys	3 45	Ring Spinners, 2d h'nd	9 00
Slubbers	4 80		
Overseers of Carding	18 72	Ring Spinners, 3d h'nd	5 50
Section Hands	11 40	Ring Spinners, girls	4 30
Second Hands	10 00		
Overseers of Spinning	19 45	Do spare hnds, g'ls	3 90

Occupations.	Average Weekly Wage, Gold Stnd'rd 1878. $	Occupations.	Average Weekly Wage, Gold Stnd'rd 1878. $
Doffers, boys & girls....................	2 42	Winders, women	5 94
Doffers. Boy.s......	2 80	Winders, overseers.............	18 00
Fly & J'k Fr'm T'ndrs.................	5 80	Weavers,..............	5 88
Reel'g & Warp'g, ov'rs.....................	15 00	Weavers, overseers.............	20 00
" second hands....	9 00	Weavers, second h'nds..................	9 00
....		Weavers, sect'n h'nds..................	9 71
" spare h'ds, girls.....................	4 20	Weavers, spare hands..................	5 25
" spoolers.............	3 96		
" do overseers.....	16 50	Weavers, 4 looms..................	3 96
" young persons..	3 00	Weavers, 5 looms..................	4 50
....		Weavers, 6 looms..................	5 01
Slasher-tenders..	9 79		
Thread-dressers.	7 95	Weavers, 8 looms..................	6 30
Drawers..............	5 55	Bobbin-boys........	4 50
Drawers, second h'nds....................	12 08	Cloth-room, overseers.............	17 25
Drawers, sect'n hands..................	8 34	Cloth-room, sec'd h'ds............	9 30
Drawers, third hands..................	6 90	Cloth-room, men	6 45
Drawers, room hands..................	6 00	....	
Quillers...............	3 67	Cloth-room, wm. & b'ys..................	4 27
Twisters..............	9 00		
Twisters, women.................	5 00	Packing-room, g's & b's.............	4 70
Winders...............	11 33		

Occupations.	Average Weekly Wage, Gold Stnd'rd 1878. $	Occupations.	Average Weekly Wage, Gold Stnd'rd 1878. $
Dyers	8 13	Men	13 60
Bundlers	8 88	Women	5 17
Overseers of Repairs	20 00	Boys	4 53
		Laborers	6 00
Mechanics	10 72	*Dressmaking.*	
Mechanics' Laborers	6 94	Managers	12 19
		Dressmakers	7 43
Engineers	11 37	*Envelopes.*	
Firemen	8 33	Cutters	16 50
Overseers of Yard	16 05	Trimmers	10 86
		Folders, women	6 75
Yard Hands	6 32	Machine hands, wm'n	6 75
Watchmen	8 12		
Teamsters	8 01	Overseer of Ruling	15 00
Cutlery.			
Forgers	12 00	Rulers, women	4 50
Forgers' helpers	6 00	Printers	9 60
Grinders	11 65	Printers, women	3 00
Sawyers	9 00	Box-makers, women	8 00
Hafters and Finishers	10 62		
		Sewers, women	9 00
Hafters & Fin'rs boys	3 30	Packers	9 75
		General Help	4 50
Machinists	14 25	Laborers	6 00
Packers	6 00	Foremen	21 00
Inspectors	10 50	*Glass.*	
Inspectors, women	7 50	Blowers	12 00
		Kiln-men	10 50
Stampers, boys & girls	9 00	Cutters	9 00
		Polishers	12 00

Occupations.	Average Weekly Wage, Gold Stnd'rd 1878. $	Occupations.	Average Weekly Wage, Gold Stnd'rd 1878. $
Gaffers	20 00	Cutters and boarders	8 40
Servitors	13 00	Winders	6 60
Foot-makers	11 00	Knitters	6 85
Pressers	13 00	Twisters	6 00
Gatherers	12 00	Sewing-girls	6 00
Stickers-up	8 00	Menders	5 70
Ware-wheelers	6 00	Rotary-knitters, men	15 00
Engravers	12 00		
Mixers	12 00	Engineers	12 00
Men, not in deprtm'ts	10 50	Yard hands & watch'n	7 80
Boys	4 50	*Leather.*	
Women and girls	4 00	Liners and Beamers	11 00
Hosiery.		Tanners	8 60
Overseer of Carding	13 50	Shavers	15 00
Young persons, card'g	6 00	Finishers	11 00
		Splitters	16 00
Overs'r, bl'chg & dye'g	16 62	Knife-men	13 50
Men, ble'ch'g & dye'g	7 87	Table-men	8 00
		Foremen	20 00
Overseer of Spinning	13 50	*Linen Goods.*	
Men & boys, spinning	6 75	Hacklers	6 75
		Preparers	6 15
Shapers	7 50	Preparers, boys	3 30
Finishers, women	5 10	Preparers, women	5 45
		Preparers, girls	3 09
		Bleachers	6 80

Occupations.	Average Weekly Wage, Gold Stnd'rd 1878. $	Occupations.	Average Weekly Wage, Gold Stnd'rd 1878. $
Finishers.............	7 50	Yard hands..........	8 10
Spinners..............	5 18	*Machines & Machinery.*	
Spinners, boys....	3 00	Pattern Makers..	15 24
Spinners, girls....	3 00	Iron Moulders....	12 30
Spinners, women.................	4 80	Brass Moulders..	13 25
		Core Makers.......	6 00
Spinners, men....	11 40	Blacksmiths........	12 15
Ruffers................	5 70	Blacksmith's helpers................	7 70
Spoolers..............	1 80		
Warpers..............	5 40	Machinists..........	13 05
Dressers..............	7 50	Cleaners and Clippers...............	7 50
Winders..............	3 55		
Machine boys......	3 90	Chuckers.............	9 75
Mechanics...........	10 09	Fitters.................	10 66
Jute Goods.		Polishers.............	9 75
Carders...............	6 00	Setters-up...........	12 00
Weavers..............	6 78	River-heaters, boys.....................	5 00
Rovers.................	3 90		
Drawers..............	4 20	Riveters..............	12 00
Feeders................	5 40	Wood-workers.....	10 39
Bundlers..............	4 50	Painters...............	8 00
Callenderers.......	7 02	Laborers..............	7 27
Batchers..............	5 70	Watchmen...........	9 00
Shifters...............	2 40	Teamsters...........	10 00
Piecers................	3 00	*Matches.*	
Bobbin carriers..	5 10	Men......................	$10 50
Winders..............	3 00	Women.................	4 00
Reelers................	4 80	Girls....................	3 00
Oilers..................	6 30	Boys.....................	3 50

Occupations.	Average Weekly Wage, Gold Stnd'rd 1878. $	Occupations.	Average Weekly Wage, Gold Stnd'rd 1878. $
Metals & Metallic Goods.		Gold-workers......	18 00
Hammers-men...	12 00	Steel-workers.....	12 00
Heaters...............	23 40	Metal-workers....	9 00
Rollers.................	13 80	Watchmen...........	10 57
Puddlers..............	18 00	Engineers............	12 00
Shinglers.............	19 50	*Millinery.*	
Helpers................	12 75	Managers............	9 62
Wire-drawers......	12 75	Milliners.............	7 16
Annealers & Cleaners..............	9 90	*Musical Instruments.*	
		Case Makers.......	13 12
Ruffers................	21 60	Varnishers...........	10 12
Finishers.............	27 00	Finishers.............	14 46
Billoters..............	9 60	Mill-men..............	14 19
Stockers..............	9 60	Action-Makers....	14 09
Reelers................	10 80	Action-makers, wm'n....................	7 11
Strikers-in..........	8 10		
Brick-masons......	18 00	Tuners.................	15 00
Brick-masons' helpers................	7 95	Laborers..............	7 70
		Paints.	
Sinkers................	22 50	Foremen..............	18 50
Sinkers' helpers.	12 00	Mixers and Grinders..............	10 46
Machinists..........	14 42		
Laborers..............	7 38	Boys......................	5 41
Mt'ls & Metl'c G'ds, Fine.		*Paper.*	
Wood-workers.....	10 50	Foremen..............	26 49
Women.................	6 00	Millwrights.........	15 21
Men......................	10 50	Rag-engine tende'rs...............	10 41
Boys and Girls....	4 65		
Moulders.............	11 75	Paper-machinetend'rs..	15 25

Occupations.	Average Weekly Wage, Gold Stnd'rd 1878. $	Occupations.	Average Weekly Wage, Gold Stnd'rd 1878. $
Thresher-women	7 40	Press Feeders	6 40
		Press Feeders	6 38
Rag-cutters	8 40	Press Feeders, wom'n	5 80
Finishers	10 20		
Finishers, girls	5 27	Compositors, daily	18 28
Finishers, boys,	7 00		
Finishers' helpers	7 27	Proof Readers	25 26
		Pressmen, daily	18 11
Cutters	7 95	Book Compositors	12 87
Cutters, girls	5 00		
Bleachers	7 56	Book Comps., women,	7 22
Rag-sorters	4 53		

Rubber Goods, Elastic Fabrics.

Men on Stock	6 57	Rubber-workers	12 00
Mechanics	13 20	Rubber-workers, wmn	5 55
Engineers & Firemen	8 77	Overseer of Weavers	15 00
Laborers	6 55		

Preserved Meats, Fruits and Pickles.

		Weavers, women	5 40
Men	12 30	Dyers	7 87
Women and Girls	4 05	Dyers, Foremen	18 00

Printing.

		Sewing girls	6 30
Job Compositors	14 12	Overseer of Spoolers	15 00
Job Compositors	15 47		
Proof-readers	20 09	Spoolers, men	8 75
Proof-readers, women	11 07	Spoolers, women	4 75
		Overseer, Leather w'k	16 50
Job Pressmen	12 60	Men on Leather work	8 40
Job Pressmen	16 53		
News-work	15 11		

Occupations.	Average Weekly Wage, Gold Stnd'rd 1878. $	Occupations.	Average Weekly Wage, Gold Stnd'rd 1878. $
Boys on Leather work....................	4 37	Dyers....................	10 50
		Silk Cleaners......	3 60
Quillers, boys & girls......................	2 75	Watchmen...........	12 00
		Machinists..........	15 00
Wood-workers.....	14 25	Engineers & Firemen..............	10 50
Safes.			
Safe Makers........	12 67	*Soap and Candles.*	
Painters..............	11 11	Men......................	9 47
Helpers................	7 56	Candle Makers...	11 00
Ship-Building.		*Stone.*	
Carpenters, old work,....................	9 00	Quarrymen.........	6 80
		Paving-cutters....	6 75
Carpenters, new work....................	7 50	Stone-cutters......	12 00
		Polishers.............	9 00
Calkers, old work....................	12 00	Blacksmiths........	10 50
		Teamsters...........	9 75
Calkers, new work....................	10 50	Laborers..............	6 00
Joiners, old work....................	12 00	*Straw Goods.*	
		Bleachers............	9 00
Joiners, new work....................	9 00	Blockers..............	12 00
		Pressers..............	12 00
Painters,..............	12 00	Packer.................	12 00
Riggers................	15 00	Machine Sewers.	10 50
Blacksmiths........	9 75	Plaster-Block makers................	11 25
Silk.			
Winders...............	5 40	Whittlers.............	18 00
Doublers.............	5 40	Menders..............	7 50
Spinners..............	6 75	Tippers................	9 00
Spoolers and Skeiners..............	5 70	Trimmers............	9 00
		Wirers.................	10 50

Occupations.	Average Weekly Wage, Gold Stnd'rd 1878. $	Occupations.	Average Weekly Wage, Gold Stnd'rd 1878. $
Braid-winders.....	9 00	Dryers and Pickers................	6 00
Machinists..........	18 00		
Tobacco.		Scourers..............	5 75
Strippers.............	7 80	Carders...............	6 19
Cigar-makers......	12 75	Carders, women.	4 54
Cigar-makers, women................	9 00	Carders, wm'n, b'ys, gls...............	4 93
Packers................	18 00	Carders, young pers'ns................	4 50
Type.		Carders, boys & girls......................	4 00
Casters................	18 56		
Dressers..............	19 60	Carders, overseers.............	18 00
Not designated...	20 00		
Rubbers...............	7 27	Strippers.............	6 19
Setters.................	5 89	Strippers, boys...	4 25
Breakers..............	4 84	Strippers, boys & girls.................	3 60
Woollen Goods.		Spinners..............	7 64
Wool-sorters........	8 50	Spinners, boys....	3 00
Washers & Scourers..............	6 66	Spinners, women.................	6 15
Dyers....................	6 66	Spinners, y'ng persons................	4 50
Dryers.................	6 12		
Young Persons....	6 00	Jack-spinners.....	8 01
Dyers and Scourers..............	6 50	Jack-spinners, boys......................	3 91
Washers...............	8 15	Jack-spn'rs, y'ngper's.............	5 00
Dyers and Dryers.................	6 90	Spoolers, women	5 64
W'sh'rs, Scour's, Dry's....................	7 12	Spoolers, girls.....	4 22

Occupations.	Average Weekly Wage, Gold Stnd'rd 1878. $	Occupations.	Average Weekly Wage, Gold Stnd'rd 1878. $
Spoolers, wom'n & girls	4 60	Packers, women	5 23
		Mechanics	12 33
Dressers and Warpers	7 68	Boys and girls	3 50
		Pressmen	7 50
Dres'rs & Wrp'rs, wmn	6 73	Section hands	9 33
		Firemen	8 78
Dressers	9 18	Engineers & firemen	10 50
Dressers, men	12 75		
Weavers	7 00	Laborers	6 69
Weavers, men	9 50	Watchmen	9 41
Weavers, women	6 95	Teamsters	9 00
Weavers, men & wm'n	7 15	Engineers	18 00
Fullers	6 89	*Wool Hats.*	
Shearers	6 60	Carders	10 66
Shearers, men & boys	5 81	Carders, boys	3 70
		Carders, foremen	21 00
Shearers, men & wm'n	6 60	Carders, second hands	9 00
Shearers, boys	5 40	Dyers, first grade	12 66
Fullers, giggers, and Shearers	6 75		
		Dyers, men	9 00
Giggers	5 90	Hardeners, foremen	10 50
Burlers	6 34		
Burlers, women	4 59	Hardeners, men	9 00
Burlers, girls	3 25	Hardeners, boys	6 00
Finishers	7 08	Machine-girls	12 00
Finishers, women	4 95	Trimmers, women	7 50
Packers	7 23	Carpenters	15 00

Occupations.	Average Weekly Wage, Gold Stnd'rd 1878. $	Occupations.	Average Weekly Wage, Gold Stnd'rd 1878. $
Blockers...............	9 83	Roping tenders...	5 82
Blockers, overseers.............	21 00	Spinners..............	5 70
		Doffers................	3 30
Finishers.............	15 00	Bobbin-setters....	2 70
Plankers,.............	9 50	Dyers..................	7 14
Plankers, foremen...............	21 00	Dressers..............	14 92
		Twisters..............	14 94
Plankers, sec'nd h'nds..................	7 50	Drawers-in..........	9 18
		Sleyers................	3 90
Plankers, boys....	6 00	Weavers...............	7 02
Worsted Goods.		Section hands.....	12 12
Wool-Sorters.......	9 00	Filling-tenders....	5 58
Wool-Washers.....	7 50	Burlers................	5 40
Wool-Preparers..	7 50	Finishers.............	7 02
Wool-Combers....	7 50	Crabbers.............	7 50
Wool-Finishers...	5 04	Driers..................	7 98
Drawers..............	6 32		

LIVING EXPENSES

The above result concerning wages being arrived at, the subject of the cost of living becomes an interesting question. We present a table showing the prices of groceries, provisions, fuel, dry goods, boots, rent, and board, from 1878.

Quantities.	ARTICLES.	Average Retail Prices. Standard, Gold. 1878. $
	Groceries.	
Barrel....................	Flour, Wheat, superfine..........	8 63
Barrel....................	Flour, Wheat, family...............	7 96
Pound..................	Flour, Rye................................	3
Pound..................	Corn Meal...............................	2
Pound..................	Codfish, dry.............................	6
Pound..................	Rice..	9
Quart....................	Beans......................................	8
Pound..................	Tea, Oolong.............................	60
Pound..................	Coffee, Rio, green....................	23
Pound	Coffee, roasted.........................	26
Pound..................	Sugar, good brown..................	8
Pound..................	Sugar, coffee............................	9
Pound..................	Sugar, granulated....................	10
Gallon..................	Molasses, New Orleans...........	57
Gallon..................	Molasses, Porto Rico...............	68
Gallon..................	Syrup.......................................	86
Pound..................	Soap, common..........................	7½
Pound..................	Starch......................................	9
	Provisions.	
Pound..................	Beef, roasting...........................	14
Pound..................	Beef, soup................................	5
Pound..................	Beef, rump steak.....................	20
Pound..................	Beef, corned............................	8
Pound..................	Veal, fore-quarter....................	10
Pound..................	Veal, hind-quarter...................	15
Pound..................	Veal, cutlets.............................	20
Pound..................	Mutton, fore-quarter..............	10
Pound..................	Mutton, leg..............................	17
Pound..................	Mutton Chops..........................	18
Pound..................	Pork, fresh...............................	10

Pound	Pork, salted	9
Pound	Hams, smoked	12
Pound	Shoulders, corned	9
Pound	Sausages	11
Pound	Lard	10
Pound	Mackerel, pickled	12
Pound	Butter	25
Pound	Cheese	12
Bushel	Potatoes	97
Quart	Milk	5
Dozen	Eggs	25

Fuel.

Ton	Coal	6 45
Cord	Wood, hard	6 74
Cord	Wood, pine	5 04

Dry Goods.

Yard	Shirting, 4-4 brown	7
Yard	Shirting, 4-4 bleached	9
Yard	Sheeting, 9-8 brown	9
Yard	Sheeting, 9-8 bleached	11
Yard	Cotton Flannel	14
Yard	Ticking	17
Yard	Prints	7
Yard	Satinet	54

Boots.

Pair	Men's heavy	3 24

Rents.

Month	Four-rooms tenement	5 55
Month	Six-rooms tenement	9 43

Board.

Week	Men	4 19
Week	Women	2 63

ADVICE TO THOSE SEEKING NEW HOMES.

"GO WEST, YOUNG MAN. "—Horace Greeley.

WHO MAKES THEIR HOMES HERE?

For some years after the late civil war, emigration from Europe increased, and the average number of arrivals of immigrants for the port of New York alone for the years 1865-1873 was 240,000. In all about 4,612,000 immigrants have arrived in this country since 1861. The past falling off in immigration was due to several causes; the depression in finances from 1873 to 1878 had caused many business failures, and the reduction in values had almost paralyzed manufacturing. Our agricultural crops were sold at very low prices because there was not a large demand for them from Europe, the cereals of Southern Russia being marketed at a lower price. As our condition improved, and business grew more brisk, the state of affairs in Europe became rapidly worse; in Great Britain the indebtedness in India was crushing the wealthy firms engaged in that trade; the demand for their manufactures from other countries was rapidly diminishing, and our goods were taking their place. There was little demand for British iron and steel: the goods of Manchester and Sheffield remained on their shelves, and American goods of better quality were offered at lower prices. The failure of the Bank of the City of Glasgow in October, 1878, of the West of England Bank in December caused great numbers of failures; and the strikes which followed the attempt of the manufacturers, ship builders and mine owners to reduce wages, added to the general gloom. It bore with great severity on the working classes and there was great room for apprehension; the tendency to emigration is a natural consequence of that apprehension.

On the Continent the condition of things was not much better. Germany, Italy, Spain and France were in a condition of upheaval.

Socialism on the one side and Ultra-montanism on the other are threatening the peace of all four, and attempts at repression only aggravate the difficulty. Russia is permeated by Nihilism, the worst form of socialism, because it is only destructive, with no desire or intention of reconstruction. Turkey is in a deplorable state, but her people do not migrate westward. From the other countries named, as well as from the Scandinavian States, the probabilities are strong of a greater immigration to this country than we have ever seen. Neither Canada nor Australasia offer any such inducements to the industrious and peace-loving immigrants as we can offer – and we shall, unquestionably, receive the larger portion of them.

But it is not alone for European emigrants that we have collected this information. Since 1873 more than two million American citizens have migrated from the Eastern States to the States and Territories west of the Mississippi; and perhaps as many more, most of them mechanics and young farmers, though including also other professions and trades, are fully determined to go within the next year or two. There is a grand field for development in the West, and the greater the number of intelligent, industrious and patriotic American citizens who shall settle its vast prairies and carry thither the religious, literary and political institutions which have caused the East to prosper in the past, the stronger our lands will be.

To both classes, then – the emigrants from foreign lands and our own sons, brothers and friends – who are setting their faces westward, we give some friendly advice to those who are intending to come and make their homes in our country:

1. We would say, first, to all intending emigrants, whether from our own or foreign countries, **do not go West without some ready money** beyond your traveling expenses, and the amount necessary to secure your lands. If you are intending to be farmers, you will need money to stock your farm, to buy seed and food for your stock, and to support your family until you can realize on your first crop. The emigrant who is thus unprovided will fare hard in a new country, though the settlers there are as generous and helpful as they can be.

The larger the amount of ready money an emigrant can command, the more easily and pleasantly will he be situated. The building of a rude house, and furnishing it in the plainest way, will consume considerable money. The man who can go to any of the western States or Territories and take up a farm and have on hand $1,000 (£200) – after paying the necessary fees and land expenses – will be well situated for the future. The man who has a much smaller sum will find that he has many hardships to undergo, and will do better to seek employment as a hired laborer for the first year, purchasing his land meanwhile, and if possible, getting in a crop.

A note on trades

The mechanic or operative who goes West for a home also needs capital, though perhaps not as much. A good carpenter, mason, blacksmith, miller, sawyer, stone-cutter, brickmaker, painter and glazier will be reasonably sure of remunerative work very soon; but $300 at least, and as much more as they can command, will be needed. The clergyman may have a congregation to preach to, but the salary he will receive from them at first will be very small, and unless he can derive at least a part of his salary from other sources, he will be very sure to suffer. The physician will find his services in demand but many of his fees will be collected with difficulty. The lawyer may have to wait long for business, but will generally manage to get his pay for his services. The editor, the artist, the bookseller, and the dealers in luxuries generally must wait till society reaches its second stage of development.

2. **Be deliberate in the choice of a location**, and do not decide until you have carefully weighed all the advantages and disadvantages of each. It is not necessary to go to the West in order to find land at a reasonable price, in good and healthy locations, and within moderate distance of a good market.

In *Maine* there are large tracts of very fair land, with ready access by river or railroad to good, though not large, markets. The soil is not as rich as that at the West, and the winters are long and cold; the climate is healthy, except a strong tendency to pulmonary consumption, which is the scourge of most cold climates on the seaboard; but these lands compare very well with the new Canadian lands, and are more accessible to markets. Wheat, rye and barley can be grown to advantage, but the summers are not generally long enough for Indian corn. The long winters make the rearing of cattle and sheep less profitable than in southern regions. The other New England States have but little land which would be attractive to emigrants.

The State of New York has much desirable land for settlers. The eastern two-thirds of Long Island has a light, friable soil, easily cultivated, inclined to be sandy, but yielding very large crops when properly manured. Railroad lines give it speedy access to the New York and Brooklyn markets, the best on the Continent. Much of this land is purchasable at from three to ten dollars an acre, and for market gardening from 10 to 20 acres is sufficient. The climate is mild and healthful, and the prompt returns for labor are sure. The difficulties in regard to this region in the past have been due to the want of good railroad communication; but these have now disappeared, and the railroads will multiply from year to year.

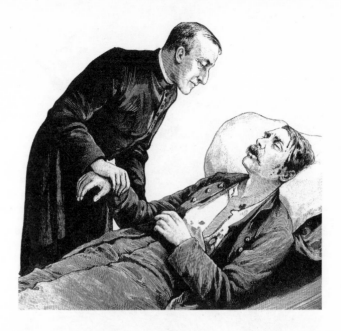

Within ten years these lands will increase in value, certainly five fold and possibly ten fold.

In the northern part of the State there is a vast tract known as the John Brown Tract, covering the greater part of several large counties, of excellent farming lands, much of it forest, with numerous lakes and streams – valuable land for grain crops, especially wheat, barley, rye, oats and buckwheat, and much of it excellent grazing land. It has been proposed to set it apart as a public park, with a view to the utilization of its lakes and streams for the supply of the canals and the upper waters of the Hudson. There are railroads and navigable streams on all sides of this vast tract, but as yet no railroad through it, though this difficulty would be readily overcome if it were fairly opened for settlement. There is much wild game in the tract, deer especially, and feathered game of all sorts, and delicious fish in great abundance. There are some bears, catamounts, lynxes, badgers, and many foxes, woodchucks, rabbits, squirrels, &c., &c. Here, land can be purchased at from 50 cents to $5 per acre.

West Virginia. Perhaps the most desirable region for some classes of settlers. The region is hilly and parts of it too mountainous for cultivation, but wherever it can be cultivated the soil is rich and productive. The whole region abounds in valuable timber black walnut, oak, ash, beech, hickory, chestnut, and other hard woods, with a fair proportion of hemlock and pine, which command high prices. Its mineral wealth of coal, petroleum, salt, lime, &c., is inexhaustible – and the markets of Cincinnati, Pittsburgh, Richmond, Norfolk and Baltimore are easily accessible from nearly all points of the State. Three railroads cross the State, one at its northern border, one at its southern, and one nearly through the centre. The Ohio River also skirts the border of the State on the north-west and is navigable for large steamers. The climate is excellent. Land can be purchased in this State at from $3 to $10 per acre, and tracts not so desirable at lower prices.

In the *Southern Atlantic States* there is a fine climate and much good land offered at reasonable prices, but, with the exception of Florida, the social, political, educational and financial conditions of these States are not such as to make emigration to them desirable. The only way in which emigration to Virginia, North Carolina, South Carolina, Georgia, Alabama, Mississippi, Louisiana, or Arkansas is practicable, is by colonies; and in most of those States, there would still be difficulties and disabilities which would make a residence there unpleasant. They are ruled too much by the pistol, the rifle, and the shot-gun, to make life agreeable there.

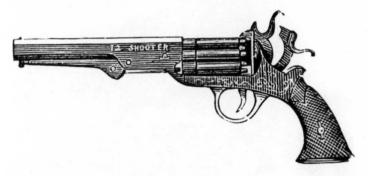

Florida is obtaining a large population of northern settlers, and though some portions of the State are subject to malarious fevers, and its principal towns suffer occasionally from yellow fever, the climate in the interior is delightful, and the culture of the orange, lemon and fig, and other semi-tropical fruits, is becoming large and profitable. Lands in desirable portions of the State are much in demand.

Texas has, since 1870, been a favorite resort for those emigrants who desire a warm climate. For rearing cattle, sheep and horses, its advantages are superior to those of any other State. The lands are very fertile and yield immense crops of Indian corn, sorghum, sugar-cane, cotton, rice and tobacco. The best mode of settlement here is by colonies, and the region to be settled should be carefully explored by a committee of the colonists in advance.

Western Texas is very dry, and along the Mexican and northern borders, Mexican raiders, and Apache and Comanche Indians very often make plundering expeditions, carrying off horses and cattle, and destroying property and *occasionally* murdering the settlers. The finances of the State are not so well administered as they should be, and the taxes are largely in arrears. Land can be obtained, unimproved, at from $1 to $5 per acre.

Tennessee (East Tennessee in particular) has much desirable land. The valleys along the Appalachian chain have a delightful climate, mineral wealth, valuable timber, and in many places a fertile soil. For capitalists, miners, workers in iron, copper or zinc, colliers, and the mechanical trades generally, this region gives better promise of obtaining a competence than most. A number of large colonies from Great Britain have already located themselves here. The financial condition of the State is not good, and the party in power have shown a proclivity for repudiation of their past debts, which has given them a bad reputation abroad. Middle and Western Tennessee raise large quantities of cotton, Indian corn and peanuts, as well as sorghum, wheat, barley, oats, &c. Land can be obtained at low prices, especially if purchased for colonies in large tracts.

Arkansas has in its western portion large tracts of very fair land, hilly but productive, and with great mineral wealth. The mountains are well covered with heavy timber. The climate is salubrious and especially adapted for those having any tendency to pulmonary diseases. Rheumatic and gouty diseases are much benefited by the Hot Springs. Yet the social, political and financial condition of the State is such that we hesitate to recommend it as a home for emigrants.

Missouri has many tracts of land suited for emigrants but we must, until she repeals her repudiation laws, regard her as an undesirable State for residence. Mechanics and machinists will often find in St. Louis good and remunerative employment, and miners may find work in her iron, lead and coal mines.

In *Indiana, Illinois and Iowa* there are no very desirable lands belonging to the United States Government, and certainly none which could be taken under the Homestead, Pre-emption or Timber Culture laws – and very little in Wisconsin. The Illinois Central R. R., Chicago & North Western, Chicago, Rock Island & Pacific, Burlington & Missouri River, and several others have land grants and will sell alternate sections to settlers at from $6 to $10 per acre. These lands being on trunk railroad lines are, in many cases, desirable as investments.

Minnesota has fertile soil, and a magnificent future. The climate in winter is cold, but dry and uniform; in summer it is delightful. The western portion of the State is the best land for Spring wheat in the United States, and the larger portion of the Minnesota wheat, which has a world-wide reputation, is raised there. This region is attracting great numbers of immigrants, and is traversed by several railroads – the Northern Pacific, and the railroad now building through the Red River Yalley from Pembina southward, are the most important. Lands every way desirable can now be procured in this region. Considerable portions of the State are well adapted to grazing, but the cattle and sheep must be carefully housed during the long winter, and hence the cost of raising stock for food purposes is greater than in most Southern States and Territories. Butter, cheese and wool are largely produced, and with much profit. The principal cities and towns have had a very rapid but healthy growth, and are good places for industrious and enterprising mechanics to find abundant and remunerative employment.

Dakota Territory is one of our newest territories. An effort likely to be successful is now making to divide it and to organize from it, with perhaps the addition of a small portion of Wyoming and Montana Territories, a new territory to be called Lincoln, which shall include the whole of the Black Hills region, where recent gold discoveries have built up a thriving district. This measure would work no ill to Dakota and would greatly facilitate the development of the new territory. The greater part of the settlements of the Territory of Dakota, as it will be after this new territory is organized, are in the eastern and south-eastern portions. The north-eastern counties are in the fertile valley of the Red River of the North, and are admirably adapted to wheat culture. South-eastern Dakota has

also a very rich soil, and is equally well suited for grazing, and the culture of cereals or root crops. There is a railroad to Yankton, the capital, in the south-east, and several others projected but not finished; there is also the Northern Pacific Railroad just below the 47th parallel and crossing the territory from east to west. The Missouri River is navigable through nearly the whole of its extent in the territory, for steamers.

Nebraska is one of the newer States of the Union, and

the population increase by immigration alone, in the year ending June 30, 1878, was not less than 100,000. The climate is excellent, though the heat of summer is sometimes intense for a few days, and the winds in winter sweep over the prairies with great force. Western Nebraska is subject to drought, the rainfall being comparatively small. Much of the country is admirably adapted to grazing purposes and with a few weeks shelter cattle can obtain their own living from the prairie grass. Portions of the State have suffered from the grasshopper or locust plague, but it is believed that the measures proposed for their repression will be found effective. The Colorado beetle or potato bug, which threatened at one time the destruction of that valuable tuber, is now regarded with indifference. Northwestern Nebraska offers less inducements for settlers than the rest of the State. It is dry and sandy, and the soil is covered in summer with alkaline deposits. Water is scanty, and many of the small lakes or ponds are saline or alkaline.

Kansas lies, in some sense, at the heart of the North American Continent. Its population is now probably not less than 730,000. The climate is healthful and pleasant, occasionally the heat is intense in summer and the average rainfall especially in Western Kansas is somewhat less than is desirable. Much of the soil is very fertile, and the profuse planting of trees has so much increased the rainfall, that these lands bid fair to yield excellent wheat and barley crops. Its crops of Indian Corn rank third or fourth in the Union, and the Wheat crops seventh or eighth. Its soil is well adapted to the growth of cereals and root crops, while it has excellent facilities for stock-raising. Though for so new a state it is traversed by an unusual number of railroads, and all portions except the north-west are readily accessible by means of the great lines, yet southern and south-western Kansas seem to be at present the regions most sought by settlers. Like its neighbors in the north and west, Kansas has had its visitations of drought, of grasshoppers or Rocky Mountain locusts, and of Colorado beetles, but has survived them all. It is hardly probable that it will be desolated by either of these scourges again very soon. The educational advantages of both Nebraska and Kansas are excellent, and the two states are in a good financial condition. The principal towns in Kansas are thriving and growing rapidly, and offer good opportunities of employment to industrious and intelligent mechanics.

Colorado is the latest accession to the sisterhood of states, having been received in 1876. It is a mountain state; the Rocky Mountains in two nearly parallel ranges, pass through it from north to south. The mountain peaks rise to an altitude of from 12,000 to 15,000 feet. On the western portion of the state beyond the Rocky Mountains, the surface is exceedingly rough, though with some beautiful valleys. This is one of the new mining regions, and gold and silver are found in paying quantities by those who are willing to undergo the hardships of the way and the still greater hardships which attach to the miner's life in such a region.

Another peculiar feature of Colorado is its vast natural parks, the largest being the North, the Middle, the South and the San Luis Parks. They are extensive fertile valleys, surrounded by the lofty mountain walls of the Rocky Mountains, and their whole surface is covered with a rich and abundant herbage, and in the season, with the gayest flowers.

Colorado has much good soil, but is better adapted to grazing than to the culture of the cereals and root crops. Its grasses are eagerly sought by cattle and sheep, and both thrive and fatten on them. Most of the arable lands require irrigation, for which, in many sections, provision has been made, and if properly irrigated, the lands yield almost incredible crops. To the enterprising farmer with a small capital, perhaps no portion of the west offers a better opportunity of profitable investment and labor. As from the salubrity, dryness and elevation of the country, Colorado has become a favorite resort for invalids, the towns form excellent markets for produce. Eastern Colorado is well provided with railroads, but as yet the principal range of the Rocky Mountains in the State has not been crossed, and Western Colorado has no railroads in operation. The recent discoveries of gold and silver in enormous quantities at Leadville, Silver Cliff, Rosita, and further West, are producing a stampede in that direction, and will compel the quick completion of railroads now in progress.

Wyoming Territory is crossed by the Rocky Mountains, covering a breadth of more than 200 miles, though between the ranges there are some fine, arable valleys, especially those of Big Horn River, and the north fork of the Platte River. A small portion of the Black Hills region, now noted for its gold mines, is in the north-east of this Territory, and the Yellowstone National Park, containing the most wonderful natural curiosities in the world, is in the north-west corner. The mineral wealth of Wyoming is less abundant than that of some of the other States, though gold in paying quantities is produced at several points. Copper is found at several points, but awaits development. There are, also, iron, lead and gypsum in large quantities. But the most profitable mineral product of the country is coal. Wyoming is better adapted to the raising of cattle than to the culture of grain and root crops. In many quarters there is a good hay crop, but for cereals or roots, irrigation is required, and in valleys, with this aid, large crops are raised. The rush of travel toward Yellowstone National Park will make the stations on the route

thither excellent markets for all kinds of produce. The Indians in the Territory are generally peaceful and friendly.

Montana Territory lies north and north-west of Wyoming, extending to the boundary of the Dominion of Canada on the north and extending to the western-most range of the Rocky Mountains on the west. It is a mountainous country, though it has many beautiful and some fertile valleys. The Territory is well watered, with the sources of the largest rivers of the continent. The climate is mild and temperate except on the high elevations. The rainfall is from 12 to 16 inches annually, but the facilities for irrigation are generally good. It is rich in mineral wealth, 120 millions of dollars of gold and silver, mostly gold, having been produced in its mines since 1861. The yield in 1878 exceeded $5,000,000. There are also valuable copper ores, coal beds, (lignite) and petroleum springs in this Territory. About one-ninth of the whole land in Montana has been surveyed; much of the Territory is unsurveyable, and worthless for agricultural and pastoral purposes. However, the sage-brush lands, covered with alkali and formerly supposed to be worthless, prove, with moderate irrigation, the most fertile lands for cereals in the world. The wheat and oats produced on these lands, surpass all

others in the market in weight and quality. But it is especially adapted for stock raising, and has already very large herds and flocks. The returns in 1878 show 300,000 cattle and 100,000 sheep, about 40,000 horses and mules. There are no railroads as yet, but it is very accessible by the Missouri and Yellowstone, and has good wagon roads. The Indians are not likely to be very troublesome.

Idaho Territory is of irregular form, narrow at the north and broad at the south, its eastern boundary being the Bitter Root and Wind River range of the Rocky Mountains. It is for the most part in the Valley of the Snake or Lewis River, the main tributary of the Columbia River, and part of the great basin lying between the Rocky and the Sierra Nevada or Cascade Mountains, but is crossed by several considerable ranges. The climate of Idaho is temperate and mild except at the highest elevations. Much of the land requires irrigation, but under a moderate amount of irrigation it yields very large crops of cereals and vegetables. The mountain slopes are covered with heavy timber. There are considerable tracts of good pastoral lands. The mineral wealth of the Territory is very great, over 23 millions of bullion, mostly gold, having been deposited in the mint and branches, previous to July 1, 1878. The yield in 1878 was at least $1,500,000, and might be almost indefinitely increased. There is one railroad in the southern part of the Territory, the Utah, extending from the Union Pacific at Ogden, to Old Fort Hall on the Snake River. The settlement by colonies is the best method in this Territory.

Utah, "the land of the Mormons", is for the most part in a deep basin surrounded by high mountains, the Wahsatch range forming the eastern rim of the basin. East of this range the country belongs to the Rocky Mountain system. In the north-west and west the plains are alkaline, treeless and covered with sage-bush, but by irrigation, even these produce 40 to 50 bushels of wheat, 70 to 80 bushels of oats and barley, and from 200 to 400 bushels of potatoes, to the acre. The Mountains are generally covered with timber, which belongs to the California forest growth, though not attaining its great height. The climate, though dry and cool from the general elevation of the surface, is very healthy. The rainfall is somewhat more than 15 inches annually, except in the north-west. About three-fourths of the inhabitants are Mormons, a peculiar people acknowledging Joseph Smith, Brigham Young, and their successors, as their supreme religious leaders and prophets, holding many strange and crude views, practicing polygamy, and defying the authority of the United States in regard to it. The remainder of the people are not Mormons, and are engaged in mining, agriculture and other business pursuits.

Utah is very rich in minerals. Mining for the precious metals has been discouraged by the Mormons, but the yield of silver is now more than $5,000,000 a year, and considerable quantities of gold are also produced. It is richer in the best iron ores than any other portion of the United States. It has also copper, lead and sulphur in abundance, and has immense beds of both lignite and bituminous coals of excellent quality. The Union Pacific Railroad passes across the northern portion, and the Utah Railroad, 54 miles in length, extends from Ogden southward. There are 350 irrigating canals.

New Mexico, a Territory largely inhabited by Spanish Americans and the Mexican or Pueblo (village) Indians. The Staked Plain, in the south-east, is a broad, almost level, treeless and waterless plain, sterile, but where it can be irrigated, capable of yielding immense crops, and producing abundantly the mesquite, a small but very valuable and deep rooted shrub of the Acacia family. West of the Rio Grande, wherever irrigation is possible, the soil yields abundantly, grain and vegetables, while the gramma grass on the hill slopes furnishes a delicious and fattening food for cattle. The raising of cattle is likely to become the favorite agricultural pursuit in the Territory, and many portions are admirably adapted for fruit raising. The climate is unrivalled for health. The rainfall in Santa Fe is about 13 inches annually; at Mesilla, in the south part of the Territory, on the west bank of the Rio Grand, it is not quite six inches. There are two railroads entering the Territory. The Atchison, Topeka and Santa Fe comes from the east, and is now completed to Santa Fe. The Denver and Rio Grande comes from the north, and has also reached Santa Fe. The population is about 130,000; 100,000 whites and nearly 90,000 of them Mexicans, the remainder mostly from the Eastern States – there are 25 to 30,000 Indians of various races, including about 8,000 Pueblo or Village Indians, of the ancient Mexican races. Education is in a very low condition; more than three-fifths of the population cannot read or write. The public Schools and most of the private Schools are under control of the Jesuits, or other Catholic orders, and the instruction is more religious than literary. Colonies will do well in this Territory.

Arizona Territory is sandwiched between California and Nevada on the west, and New Mexico on the east, having Utah on the north, and Mexico on the south. A few artesian wells furnish a scanty supply of water, and among the ruins of the Aztec towns are large reservoirs for holding the rain water, which rarely falls. The southern part of the Territory is watered by the Gila and its numerous tributaries, and is more easily cultivated. The heat in summer in south and south-west Arizona is terrible, 120° in the shade, and 160° or more in the sun, is not an uncommon temperature in summer, but the winters are mild and delightful. Irrigation is necessary to

agricultural production everywhere in the Territory, but it contains excellent grazing lands, and a sufficient amount of arable land to insure a sufficient supply of vegetables and cereals for the population. There is considerable timber on the Mountain slopes, and the various species of cactus attain great size there. The mineral wealth of Arizona is enormous: gold, silver, quick-silver, platina, tin, nickel, very pure copper ores, lead, the best ores of iron, bituminous coals of excellent quality, salt, sulphur, gypsum and many of the precious stones, abound there. The Indians are no longer troublesome. For miners, engineers, or herdsmen, the Territory is very attractive, and intelligent farmers can do well there.

Nevada was admitted as a State when its population was notoriously too small, and though the number of inhabitants is increasing, it is still below the quota for a member of Congress, though it is represented by one member in the lower house of Congress. Its mineral wealth surpasses that of any of the western States or Territories. In 1878 the yield of silver from the mines was $47,676,863, and the silver mines are scattered over the whole State. Its production of gold, mostly parted from the silver, is nearly $20,000,000, and both gold and silver are increasing. It has also quick-silver, lead, copper, iron, antimony, sulphur, arsenic, graphite, borax, carbonate of soda, in immense quantities, rock salt, lignite or brown coal of good quality, &c., &c. The climate varies with the latitude and elevation. The cold of winter is intense in the mountains and lofty valleys, and the heat in the summer is equally intense, rising to 105° in June. In south-east Nevada, there is much less cold, and cotton and the sugar cane are both cultivated there. Southern Nevada is a barren and desolate region, but has valuable mines. The Central Pacific Railroad crosses the State in a west-south-west direction, and there are several local railroads. Nevada is a good State for miners, smelters, engineers, intelligent farmers, grazers, and enterprising mechanics.

In *California*, the climate varies through all the gradations of the temperate and semi-tropical region. The summer mean temperature has a range of 33° between Humboldt Bay and Fort Yuma, while the winter mean varies but 14°. The annual rainfall is equally varied, at Humboldt Bay, from 57 to 64 inches; in Klamath Co., from 81 to 110 inches. It is a land of lakes, rivers and mountains, with some of the most beautiful and fertile lands in the world, and some of the most desolate and forbidding. Its golden grain is famous the world over, and its vineyards and olive gardens, luscious fruits and abundant crops of every thing which will grow anywhere, are well known. For the most part, arable lands are too dear for the farmer of small means. Many of these large ranches are on unsurveyed lands, and must eventually come into market, when there will be a good opportunity for purchasing farms.

There are nearly 40,000,000 acres of grazing lands. South-east California is a wild volcanic region, with its dry lakes covered with salt or bitumen, its vast sinks, many of them below the surface of the ocean, and its Death valley, most appropriately named. It is now proposed, by a short ship canal, to turn the waters of the Pacific into this valley and render it habitable, where it is not submerged. The mineral wealth of California is very great. Its production of gold and silver since 1849 has been nearly $700,000,000. Most parts of the State are easily reached by railroads and steamers. California is a good State for artisans, gardeners, vine growers and dressers, and farmers who are content to be employed at first by others; miners, metal workers, machinists, and operators in woollen mills, &c., &c., but less so for those who wish to purchase farms.

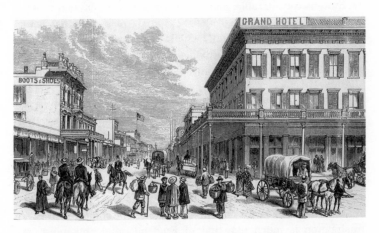

Oregon, one of the two States lying on the Pacific. Most of the State is well watered, mainly from the affluents of the Columbia and Snake. It is divided by the Cascade and Blue ranges of Mountains into three sections, known as Western, Middle, and Eastern Oregon.

Western Oregon, though broken and hilly from the presence of the coast range, is generally fertile, and the Mountains are clothed with heavy timber to their summits. The Willamette Valley, lying between the Coast and Cascade ranges, is exceedingly fertile and beautiful. The temperature is mild and delightful. Middle Oregon is dryer, not so well watered nor so fertile. The climate is agreeable, except in the south, where the high mountains make it sometimes excessively cold. Eastern Oregon is dry, but has many well watered and fertile valleys. The winters are cold, with deep snow. Western Oregon is traversed for almost its entire length from south to north by the California branch of the Northern Pacific. The rivers abound with valuable fish. The salmon fisheries send out about $10,000,000 worth annually, mostly in cans, and canned beef is also largely exported. The agricultural crops are good, and command a fair price; wheat, oats and potatoes yield largely. The timber trade is very large, the finest trees of Oregon being very large, and the wood durable. Fruit is also largely cultivated. It is an excellent country for raising live stock, especialy cattle and sheep. The wool product of the State is considerable, and mostly consumed in Oregon woollen factories. The mineral wealth of the State is very great, but not so fully developed as it should be. Miners, lumbermen, fishermen, herdsmen, and industrious, intelligent farmers, will find Oregon the best place for them. There is much Government land yet in market.

Washington Territory is, except Alaska, the extreme north-western Territory of the United States, and Alaska is not as yet, in a condition to invite immigration. Western Washington like western Oregon, has much broken land, but the valleys, especially around both sides of Puget Sound, are very fertile, and the slopes of the mountains are heavily timbered, and valuable. There are 200 miles of railroad in operation in the Territory, and the Columbia River, Snake River and Clark's Fork are navigable. The climate of Western Washington is much like that of England, mild and moist, the extreme heat of summer seldom exceeding 80° F., and the nights cool and agreeable. The winters are so mild that it is seldom necessary to house the livestock. The summers in Central and Eastern Washington are dry and hot, winters much like those of

Pennsylvania, cold, but not severe. Only about one-third of the public lands are yet surveyed, There is some gold in the Territory, but more coal, iron, and other minerals. The coal in the Puyallup Valley is anthracite, of excellent quality, and a railroad now runs to the mines. There are other beds of both anthracite and bituminous coal, along the Cascade Mountains. The soil is, much of it, very fertile, and the finest trees are but little inferior to the giant sequoias of California. The Territory is well adapted to the culture of the cereals, and it is also a good region for wool growing and stock raising. The salmon and other fisheries in Puget Sound, and in the Columbia, are very profitable. A grand future awaits the citizens of Oregon and Washington.

THE GREAT WEST

THE WEST:

WHO SHOULD MIGRATE THITHER

There have been in our country, as in other countries of Christendom, periodical crazes – times when nations, states, and communities were completely under the influence of a single dominating idea, which drove out all other ideas and thoughts from their minds. Eating or drinking, waking or sleeping, they could think and talk of nothing else. These crazes sometimes seem very absurd to us, as we look back upon them; but at the time, they are intensely real. They may do some good, but they do much evil also. They may be industrial, scientific after the fashion of popular science, political, agricultural, educational, or religious; but whatever may be the subject of the craze, its effect is much the same.

AMERICANS SUBJECT TO MANIAS

The Morus Multicaulis Craze

The Morus Multicaulis fever of 1835–38 was an example of the agricultural and industrial sort. Men of sound judgment and of good business abilities, were deluded into the belief, that by planting or starting a half-dozen cuttings of a foreign shrub or tree they would speedily amass an immense fortune; that from these little sticks, not so large as a pipe stem, there would presently grow stately mulberry-trees, on which millions of silkworms to be somehow procured, would feast and form cocoons, which any girl could reel, and which would, by some hocus-pocus process, be transmuted into elegant dress-silk, dress-goods, velvets, satins, ribbons, and lace, all of which would be furnished without cost, to the fortunate possessor of the mulberry slips.

The whole thing looks supremely ridiculous to us now; but then, every man and woman invested all that they could earn, or beg, or steal in these precious twigs; and when the bubble burst, as it did in 1837, it involved millions of people in heavy, and some of them in ruinous losses.

The Second Advent Craze of 1843

There followed this a religious delusion, the Second Advent craze of 1843, when people made up ascension robes, and some in their zeal stole the muslin which they used in their manufacture.

The Western Craze of 1847–48

A few years later there was an emigration craze. The West, which then meant Indiana, Illinois, Michigan, Wisconsin, Iowa, and Missouri, and the cities of Chicago, Milwaukee, and St. Louis, was on every man's lips; tens of thousands of miles of railroads were projected, thousands of cities laid out on paper, stocks and bonds issued without stint, every kind of wild-cat paper issued as money, and the most fabulous stories told, of the fortunes amassed in a single day, by the advance in lands, city lots, and stocks. This craze, too, died out from sheer absurdity, but with frightful losses.

Other Crazes

Time would fail me to tell of the crazes since that time; of the petroleum mania, the shoddy speculation, the mining fever of a dozen years ago, the new railroad excitement, all ending in general disaster, and in long years of gloom; now to be replaced, perhaps, by an emigration fever, and a reckless speculation in mining properties, almost as absurd as the earlier manias, and even more disastrous. It seems to be the fate of the Yankee to be at one moment on the top of Pisgah, and the next in the Valley of Humiliation.

The present Mining Craze

There are at the present time (May, 1880) over 1500 mining companies or organizations in the region west of the Mississippi, nine tenths of them formed within two years past, and having a nominal capital of about \$2,000,000,000. From ignorance of the business, bad management, and often from misrepresentation in regard to their value, more than nine tenths will prove unproductive, and the stockholders will meet with heavy losses. One hundred and forty mining companies, incorporated in San Francisco within a few years past, have assessed their stockholders \$47,000,000, besides their original capital, and have paid in all only \$6,000,000.

THE DESIRE TO GO WEST — EMIGRATION FEVER

"But," it may be asked, "what has all this to do with going West?" Much more than you may think, my friend. You are a working-man, a machinist, an operative in a manufactory, a builder, or an artisan in some one of the trades or callings which are followed in our Eastern communities, or you have been farming in a moderate way, or engaged in trade. You have laid up a little, have perhaps a home of your own, though there may be a small mortgage on it; but you do not get rich so fast as you would like, and, as you look upon your wife and little ones, you think to yourself, "I have not much to leave to them if I were taken away, and they might be left to suffer. I must try in some way to accumulate property faster, so as to be able to leave them in better circumstances." As you look about you, there seems to be no chance in your present circumstances and position, for doing this. If you are a working-man, your wages are only likely to be advanced, when there are such advances in food and clothing and living expenses, as will leave you no more net gain than you have had in the past. If you are following a trade or calling, any advance in price is necessarily accompanied by an advance in material, or wages of employees, and in living expenses, which leaves you no better off than you were before. In trade, there is perhaps a little advantage in prosperous times, because there are not so many bad debts, but very few can lay up money in retail trade. You are apparently cut off from any considerable improvement of your circumstances.

Meantime, the spirit of emigration is abroad in the air. Every other man whom you meet is talking of the West – *the West*, with its rich and constantly developing mines of gold and silver; the West, with its productive farms and its agricultural wealth; the West, with its immense herds of cattle, and its hundreds of thousands of sheep and goats. You ask yourself, "Why not go to this great West and accumulate wealth, as others have done, in a few years, instead of wasting my time here for a mere pittance?" The mania is abroad, and you are in a fair way to become one of its victims. Still your question is a reasonable one. Allow us to answer it, after the Yankee fashion, by asking some others. Have you a very clear, distinct idea of what is included in emigration to a new State or Territory?

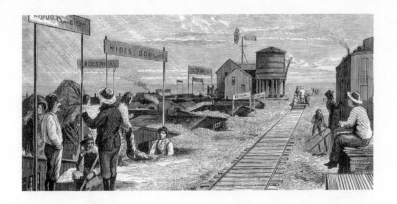

The Discomforts

You have a good, comfortable home, with all its appliances and conveniences. It may be small, but it is a good home. If you emigrate to the frontier, even if you have a good sum of money to pay your living expenses, your home for the first year or two must be of sods, of logs, or of canvas. You must content yourself with the fewest possible conveniences for comfortable housekeeping, and the roughest and poorest food; all those thousand little comforts, which go to make up our Eastern civilization, will be wanting, for a year or two at least. If you make your new home on the prairie, the summer's sun will scorch and burn you, and the winter's snow may bury your little cabin out of sight. Neighbors at first will be few and far apart. Schools and churches will come in time, but you will have to lift heavily to make them come, and for a year or two you will be obliged to go without them. If your home is in the timbered land, other disabilities, equally severe, will try you.

Wolves, panthers, lynxes, and now and then a bear, will pay you visits, not so much because they care for your society, as because they hope to find some food, on or about your premises. You will have a vigorous appetite, though it may sometimes be difficult to satisfy it; and the exposure to the pure open air may improve your health, though there are some chances of malarial fever or catarrhal affections. You may have been particular about your clothing at the East, but you will very soon present an appearance which would well befit a tramp.

Dangers to Health

We do not speak of the risks to health, because, with only a few exceptions, the region west of the Mississippi is healthy. The region bordering immediately on the Mississippi, from the Iowa line southward, and the lower Missouri, as well as Southeast Kansas, much of the Indian Territory and the lower lands of Texas, are to some extent subject to bilious, remittent, and intermittent fevers, and care should be taken, if a location is sought there, to select elevated lands, with good drainage and no standing water, and to avoid the night air and heavy dews.

Risks of Loss

There are also some risks in investing the money you have been able to save in the past. If you have saved $1,000 or $2,000, and buy or secure a farm in some one of these new States or territories, it will probably be about twenty months before you can realize anything on your first crop. Meantime you must make your first payments on your land, pay for having it broken up, which will cost you from four to eight dollars per acre, according to the thoroughness with which it is done; must pay for seed, and buy the horses, mules, oxen, or cows needed, and the wagons, carts, ploughs, harrows, cultivators, and, if you can, a harvester for your first grain crop. You must also buy or build your cabin and furnish it, or, which will be about the same thing, pay the freight on your furniture from the East. And whatever you or your family need in the way of food or clothing, before you receive anything from the first crop, must also come out of this reserve.

The Chances of Success and Failure

It is true that, if you are successful, your money will have been put out at good interest – ten, twelve, or even twenty per cent, perhaps – but there are chances of failure, and the risk should be fairly considered. Even if you are able to pre-empt your land, and so delay paying the Government price for it for thirty-three months, or take it up under the Homestead or Timber Culture acts, or buy it of the railway companies, on long time, you will still find ample use for your $1,000 or $2,000 in paying your necessary expenses, and maintaining your family, until the crop money comes in.

What a Successful First Crop will Accomplish

If this first crop has been twenty acres in root crops and twenty in wheat (you will hardly be able to crop more than forty acres at first), and there have been no drawbacks, but a full crop of both, you should be able to raise about $2,000 from the forty acres, and cultivating besides a large garden plot, to provide your family with all the vegetables they need. A pig and a calf will add to your meat rations, and your cow should furnish the butter and milk needed. Under these circumstances, if you are a good manager, you may be able to make your next payment, if necessary, on your farm; to improve your dwelling, and break up an additional twenty or forty acres; support your family in better style than the previous year, and still lay up a small sum toward replacing your reserve.

The Possibilities of Failure

But suppose that your wheat is consumed while growing, by the grass-hopper or Rocky Mountain locust, and your root crops by the Colorado beetle or potato bug, and the gophers, or the moles; or that your farm is desolated by drought; that your horses or mules, your oxen or cows, or the pig or pigs, whose luscious flesh you have been looking forward to, as a part of your winter's supply, are destroyed by wolves, lynxes, or bears, or are seized with the diseases not

infrequently prevalent; your supplies for the coming year will be cut off, and if your reserve has all been expended, you will be very hard pressed to find the means for supporting your family, and obtaining the seed necessary to be planted or sown for the next year. You may say that it is not probable that all these disasters will come at once; so would have said many thousands of farmers, who put in their first or second crops in the autumn of 1873 or the spring of 1874, and yet it was exactly these disasters which did come in that year, and thousands of families were only kept from starvation, by the public and private bounties bestowed upon them, largely by Eastern people.

Rose-colored pictures of the Emigration Agents

This is not the sort of talk you will be likely to hear from the agents of emigration societies, or land-grant railroad companies; they will represent to you that the climate, soil, and productions render the country a perfect paradise; that there are no disturbing or discouraging influences, but that everything is perfectly lovely. The crops are grown without labor, the houses are built without effort, the livestock takes care of itself, the rain irrigates thoroughly the long-parched soil, so soon as the immigrant plants his foot upon it. Such unthinking advocates of emigration will accuse us of hostility to it, but most unjustly; for while we have presented frankly and without exaggeration the troubles and privations which the emigrant must encounter in the early months of his settlement, there is a bright future before him, if he has only the nerve, patience, enterprise, and good fortune to triumph over them all.

Why the Dark Side as well as the Bright Should be Presented

No man of true courage is ever discouraged by the presentation of difficulties to be surmounted in attaining a desired end; he is only stimulated to greater effort to overcome them. If, on the other hand, only the bright side is presented to him, and all knowledge of difficulties and discouragements is carefully withheld from him when he is called unexpectedly to encounter Serious trials and privations, of which he had no previous warning, the probability of disappointment and despair is greatly increased. He is the best friend of the emigrant who shows him what clouds and storms will darken his way, as well as the glowing sunshine which will gladden it.

What the Emigrant has to Encounter

Your warfare is not with human foes, or despotisms hastening to decay, but only with the inertia of the natural world, with the difficulties and privations incident to a new settlement, and possibly with insect foes, diseases, and summer droughts. These once overcome, you will have established yourselves in homes whose value is constantly increasing, and will have ere long an income sufficiently ample for your family and yourselves. You who are enterprising, courageous, and persevering, come forward and enlist!

The Chances for the Men who have Trades

Those working-men who have good trades, and are skilful in them, may find profitable employment in their respective lines of business much sooner than the farmer, and have an opportunity of obtaining better social positions, than they can usually do here; but they will do well to secure some land – enough for their own needs. To keep

two or three cows and a few sheep; to raise what grain and root crops are needed for home consumption; to have a comfortable home, with pleasant surroundings of flowers, shrubs, fruit and forest-trees, and a good vegetable garden, will not be very expensive, if there are young hands to help; and if in, or near one of the growing towns of the West, it will be not only a source of pleasure, but of constantly increasing profit. And in many instances there will be opportunities for the cultivation of special crops on a small scale, the raising of poultry, the rearing of silk-worms, the care of bees, etc., etc., which will add materially to the revenues of the household.

Stock-raising

We can hardly advise our friends to go into the business of stock-raising or wool-growing in the West, unless they have a considerable capital at command. A cattle-ranch, even on the smallest scale which will pay a profit, requires at least $20,000 to start, and would be more speedily profitable with $50,000. As many of the large cattle-farms or ranches are owned by joint stock companies, some stock might be taken in them with a smaller sum, say $5,000 or

$10,000; but their capital is usually from $500,000 to $1,000,000, and the dividend on a small sum would be nothing for two or three years, and not a large amount for several more. Eventually it might pay.

Becoming a Herder, or "Cow-Boy"

Another way of working into this business would be to become a herder or "cow-boy" at first; and, buying a few cows and calves, herd

them with the rest of the stock. At "rounding up" time, brand them with the herder's own brand (which must be recorded), and in the course of five or eight years there will be a herd of respectable size from this small beginning, so that it will answer to set up a separate ranch. This can be done to much better advantage in Texas than elsewhere; but the Texas cattle bring lower prices in the market than those of the States farther north.

Sheep-Farming

As to the sheep, $14,000 or $15,000 will answer to start a sheep farm if a man understands the business, though a larger sum is better. The profit from raising sheep is sooner realized than from raising cattle, and is nearly as great. A single man with a little money, who will be content to serve as a shepherd for five years, and pasture his own sheep with his employer's flock, can lead out a very respectable flock at the end of that time; but it would be difficult, if not impossible, to support a family in that way before the five years were up. The wages of a herder or a shepherd vary from $18 to $25 a month and keeping; but their lives are very lonely, and the danger to life and limb is considerable.

Great Fortunes to be Made in Mining?

There is at the present time a great craze in regard to the fortunes to be made in mining operations, especially for gold and silver in the West. You will hear every day that Mr. A. or Mr. B., Senator C., or Judge D., or Col. E. has become a millionaire, through the valuable mines in which he has invested. Sometimes you will be told that some of these fortunate men have accumulated five, six, ten, or twenty millions in a very short time. This may be true, or it may not.

If it is true, you may be sure of these three things: First, that these millionaires were men of comfortably large fortunes before they took hold of those great enterprises; that they investigated very thoroughly, and, having their money at command, took advantage of the circumstances, and bought for a small sum what has brought them a large profit. Second, that a great part of their profit has been realized by selling shares in a company which they have formed, putting in a property which cost them perhaps $80,000, as the equivalent for a capital stock of $8,000,000 to $5,000,000. The mine may have been worth five or ten times what they actually paid for it, but most of these concerns are watered prodigiously. Third, that however many millions this fortunate mine-owner may suppose himself to be worth, or make others believe he is worth, it is by no means certain, that within one, two, or three years he may find that he is not worth as much money as he was, when he made his first investment in mining property.

Even the shrewdest man who is not practically acquainted with mining, may make a great mistake in purchasing mining property. Another lesson is that you should never be beguiled into buying mining stocks, no matter at what price they may be offered. No! if you *will* put your money into mining property, wait until you can see the property for yourself; until you can learn how much ore has been taken out, what its probable value per ton is, &c &c. It is necessary also to know what is the character of the product of the mine: if it is gold, whether it is free milling gold, which needs only to be crushed by the stamps and run over the amalgamated plates to yield up the quarter part of the gold; or whether it is combined with sulphur and copper, or sulphur and zinc, or with lead. Where sulphur

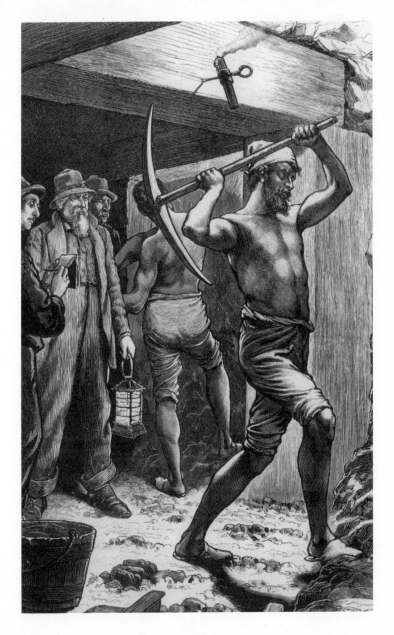

is present in the form of sulphides or sulphurets, roasting, and sometimes chlorination or lixiviation, is required to expel the sulphur; and these are costly processes, and will only pay when the ores are rich. If the ores are silver, you should know whether it is combined with lead, zinc, or copper; whether it is a carbonate, a sulphate, a chloride, a telluriate, or a sulphuret of silver, or of silver-bearing lead. Most of the silver ores require smelting, some of them roasting, some chloridinizing, and some lixiviation.

If, then, you will buy an interest in a mine, look it over thoroughly before buying; be sure to "come in on the hard pan," as the miners say, i.e., pay only the first cost of the mine, before they have begun to water the stock, and pay for the mine, only the value of the ore in sight. You cannot be badly defrauded if you do this.

The Life of the Practical Miner

Having thus briefly placed before you the difficulties and dangers incident to investments in mining property, let us say a few words concerning the life of the practical miner and his work. By the practical miner we mean here, not, necessarily, the dull, uneducated mining laborer, but in many instances the owners of new and undeveloped mines, who, with but moderate means, and with great intelligence and commendable industry, are working diligently, to open a mine and ascertain its real value. In many instances, in Colorado, Montana and Utah, graduates of our great universities, professional men, merchants, mining engineers, master mechanics, and machinists have bent their backs, begrimed their faces, and blistered their hands, at their unaccustomed toil with the pick or shovel, the winch, the pan or the sieve, in washing, amalgamating, digging shafts, opening winzes and tunnels, drawing up and lowering the miner's bucket &c &c.

This is hard work; and It is only the hope of gain sufficient to remunerate these volunteer working-men for their toil, which gives strength to their arms and vigor to their blows. For a long and steady pull, they would have to give place to the sturdy and stolid laborer; but their energy and will power may hold out, till they have sufficient encouragement in their prospects, to warrant their employment of men of greater muscle, though of less intellectual ability.

Hardships of the Immigrant to a Mining Region

The lot of the immigrant to the mining districts, even if he has a moderate capital at command, is harder, and his condition more uncomfortable, than that of the immigrant who has a farmer's vocation in view. The farmer can have a rude yet comparatively comfortable shelter from sun, wind, and storm reared very soon. His farm is on the prairie or the edge of the forest, and at all events not on broken or rocky ground. He can command generally food sufficient for himself and his family, either from the nearest town, or, if on the extreme frontier, by the use of his rifle or his fishing-rod. Before he realizes anything from his own farm, there is always opportunity for earning good wages by working for his neighbors.

But the immigrant to the mining regions finds them invariably in a rough and broken country; and if he seeks a place anywhere in the Rocky Mountain ranges, especially on their western slopes, which are richest in gold and silver, he will soon discover that he has come upon a region, which has hardly a parallel on the earth's surface in the boldness of its cliffs, the ruggedness of its precipices, the depth and gloominess of its canons, and the wonderful character

of its eroded and water-worn rocks and caverns. Sharp, treeless ridges, upheaved by earthquakes or displaced by volcanic action, are the most frequent localities of the larger fissure veins and lodes.

The Mining of Other Minerals

But gold and silver are not the only minerals to be mined in this Western country, nor the only minerals which will yield a large profit. The production of gold and silver in the United States amounts to from $80-90,000,000 a year; but it constitutes only about one twelfth of the entire mineral production of the country. The coal mines yield a much larger annual amount than the mines of gold and silver – at least three, and perhaps four, times as much. Copper, lead, and zinc are produced annually to the amount of more than one hundred millions, while iron and steel, the latter now made directly from the ore, exceed two hundred millions. The other mineral products, such as petroleum, salt, plaster of Paris, cement, sulphur, borax, nitrates and carbonates of soda and potassa, etc., etc., make up another large sum. The production and marketing of some of these minerals will yield a more certain, and in the end, a larger profit than most of the gold and silver mining.

The Artisan in the West

But it may be that you have no fancy for mining or the exploiting of mineral products. You have not been brought up on a farm, nor been accustomed to the rearing of livestock. You have a good trade, and are skilful in it, and you have been accustomed from boyhood to the care of a garden, and to the cultivation of vegetables, fruit trees, and flowers; but your present quarters are too contracted for any considerable indulgence of your tastes. You have, moreover, a great desire to go West. What shall you do? Go, by all means, friend. You will find abundant employment, and a good opportunity to acquire a competence. You may have to rough it at first, but in a short time you will find yourself in a position of comfort.

What Callings are the Most Successful

If your calling is one of the indispensable ones – builder, mason, plasterer, painter, glazier, paper-hanger, blacksmith, butcher, baker, hatter and furrier, or perhaps tanner, shoemaker, harness-maker, brick-maker, watchmaker and jeweller, bookbinder, stationer and news-dealer, miller, saw-mill tender, tinman, roofer, &c &c – you will find plenty of work in any of the new mining towns or farming villages, and at good prices; but take our advice: secure, before it is too high, a forty-acre lot of good land in the immediate vicinity, have it broken up, build a house on it, small at first, but so it can be enlarged easily. Sow your land to wheat or root crops, and you can sell this crop at home, with but little trouble, and add a comfortable amount to your income. Then plant young trees – shade trees, fruit trees of well-known and choice varieties – and devote your spare moments and hours to them; plant eight or ten acres, as soon as you can, with all the vegetables and truck which go to make up a market garden, and you will soon find that however profitable your trade may be, your market garden brings in twice as much; and your nursery of young trees will soon be thronged with purchasers.

Horticulture a Second Trade

If you have children who are growing up, add flowers, build a greenhouse, and as fast as you can learn the art of floral cultivation, work into the florist's business. If work at your trade is dull, push your flowers, your market garden, your nursery, the more, if work is brisk, train your children to attend to this, giving them your oversight as often as you can.

Following up this course, you need not break your heart if your neighbor A, who is a mine owner, finds a pocket in his mine which yields him many thousand dollars; or if your neighbor B sells out his shares for more than they cost him. You are adding to the earth's production, you are making two blades of grass grow where only one grew before, or a hundred trees where none grew previously; your neighbor who speculates in shares produces nothing; he only gambles on what others have produced. You may acquire property more slowly than he, but your course is sure and safe, and the chances are that ten years hence, you will be much the richer man of the two, though he may have won and lost a dozen fortunes in that time.

The Teacher at the West

If you are a teacher, and would better your condition by emigrating to the West, our advice would be much the same. Good teachers are always in demand, even in the newest towns. The Yankee must have a school-house, and, generally, a church too, in his new village, quite as soon as a house for himself; the school-house, at all events, is sure to come very soon, whatever the nationality of the settlers of the town. But while you are teaching the young ideas how to shoot, teach the shrubs, the young trees, and the flowers and vegetables to put forth their shoots too. Secure your forty acres as near to the town as possible, and make and keep it productive. Then, when teaching becomes a drudgery, and you desire to be relieved from its cares, you will have a valuable property, and a profitable business to make your declining years comfortable. Keep bees, if you can, or pigeons or poultry, rabbits or hares, or pet birds, anything except cats and cur-dogs. Teach your children botany and natural history, and lead their minds up from the beautiful flowers to Him who painted them with His sunbeams, and from the wise and curious animals, so well adapted to their modes of living, to Him whose omniscience guides all the actions of His creatures, and whose providence provides for their needs.

Professional men, and Clergymen

The members of the several learned professions hardly need our advice in regard to emigration. Clergymen, in the exercise of their clerical duties, will find their positions at first trying because of the present poverty of most of the settlers. When a man has expended all his means in paying for his land and its first cultivation, he cannot aid in supporting a minister, however strong may be his desire to do so. Moreover, these new immigrants must aid in building a church edifice of some kind, as well as in supporting a pastor, and this, while still straitened in regard to their own means living. After a few years this will be easy, but meantime they cannot with safety dispense with the church or clergyman. If the clergyman has any spare money he will do well to buy some land, or at least to secure the title of it to himself; it may be very convenient by and by. In most instances the Home Missionary Societies, of the different denominations, in the East will grant aid to deserving churches and ministers, till the churches are able to stand alone.

Lawyers and Physicians

Lawyers and physicians are plenty enough, but they fare rather better than clergymen. The lawyers find a great deal of business in the abundant litigation in the mining districts and in conveyancing, and most of them have an additional resource in politics, which sooner or later bring them into official positions. The physicians, beside their professional duties, are mostly chemists, metallurgists, or botanists, and find employment which is profitable, either in connection with some of the mining, assaying or smelting companies, or in a professor's chair.

Engineers and Artists

Engineers are sure of constant employment, whether mining or civil engineers, if they understand their business. Artists generally come as visitors, not immigrants, but are often employed by the wealthy mine owners very profitably.

Operatives and Employees in Factories, etc

Employees and operatives in manufactories may find employment in some kinds of manufacture in the States nearest the Mississippi, for there is a large amount of manufacturing in Minnesota, Iowa, Missouri, Nebraska, and Kansas, and manufactures are increasing in Arkansas, Louisiana, and Texas. There is some opportunity for millers, saw-mill hands, sash, door and blind makers, coopers, agricultural machinery hands, iron and steel rail makers, iron furnace and foundry hands, stove and hollow ware founders and finishers, smelters, and in California and Oregon, salmon packers and a few woollen factory hands. In Kansas, Arkansas and Texas there are some cotton factories, and many oil mills for expressing cotton-seed oil, castor oil, linseed oil, etc.

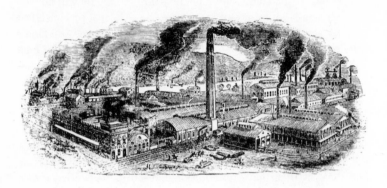

Cotton and Woollen Factories

The factories for manufacturing cotton and wool are likely to increase largely within a few years. A machine has been invented, and is now in use to some extent, for spinning cotton with the seed in it, unginned, and the yarn is much better and more beautiful and durable than can be produced from ginned cotton. The yarn produced by these machines is destined to be manufactured largely in the vicinity of the cotton fields, and will thus create a home demand for cotton. Wool is now produced so largely throughout this whole region, that much saving of freight will result from its manufacture near the centres of wool production. When this is accomplished, the operatives from Eastern cotton and woollen factories will find it for their interest to emigrate westward.

IS IT NECESSARY TO GO WEST?

But, after all, is it not barely possible that there are lands east of the Mississippi, where, all things being taken into the account, a man or family can live as well and make as much money as in the West, and

at the same time avoid the hardships and discomforts of a life on the frontier?

There is the same choice of occupations here as at the West. Land is not quite so low, generally, but on the other hand you avoid the long and expensive journey to the West. The agricultural production, under favorable circumstances, does not differ materially; but there prices are low and the cost of transportation to a better and higher market is very heavy, while here you have a market almost at your doors, and that, one which pays the highest price for produce. If there is a difference, as there certainly is in some sections, the Eastern climate is healthier, neither the heat nor the cold so oppressive, the rainfall sufficient to prevent any apprehension of a drought, the insect pests much less formidable, and the danger from malarial fevers less serious. The intensity of the cold of winter is greater in the northern tier of States and Territories of the West than in the middle Atlantic States, and the heat of the south-western States and Territories in summer, has no parallel in the East.

WHERE THE NEW EASTERN LANDS ARE

"But where," you will ask, "are these lands, to which you refer in the Atlantic States, and how can we reach them?" We answer, Not perhaps in Maine, though there is much good land in the State which is to be had at from three to five dollars per acre; but it is, for the most part, somewhat remote from good markets, and the winter's cold is severe and protracted. Yet if you wish to engage in silver or copper mining there is a very fair opportunity for doing so in Maine, and with perhaps as good results as most men will attain at the West, and with lighter expenses.

Northern New Hampshire and Vermont have some good lands to be purchased at low prices, but the winters are hard and the soil rocky. Massachusetts, Connecticut, and Rhode Island are too densely populated to have much cheap land. Still there are old farms to be bought very low in the two former states, which need only the energy of a thorough farmer, to bring them into a thrifty condition and to make them yield very profitable crops. There are more or less mines and quarries in all three, which would pay well if well managed.

Northern New York

New York has two large tracts of land and several smaller ones which, all things considered, are as favorably situated for profitable settlement as most of the Western lands. These are, first, the region known as "the Adirondacks," "John Brown's Tract," etc., in Northern New York. The country is well watered, the soil is mostly a virgin soil, with considerable timber of excellent quality on it, and will yield large crops of spring wheat, rye, and barley, the early sorghum, and in some sections Indian corn. The land can be purchased for from two to five dollars per acre, except where there is heavy timber on it, when it would probably be worth from eight to ten dollars. It is not at present traversed by any railroads, but these would soon be constructed if settlements were made there. The winter is very cold, but so it is in the valley of the Red River of the North. Wheat, rye, oats, and barley, as well as potatoes and other root crops for which it is well adapted, can be brought to market at a moderate expense, and the prices they will command are much higher than those paid in the West.

Long Island

The second region which is eligible for settlement in New York, is on Long Island, and mainly in Suffolk County. It seems almost incredible that half a million of acres of land lying between thirty-five and ninety miles from New York City, the best and most inexhaustible market in the world, with a good soil, a very healthful climate, well watered, and having a sufficient but not excessive annual rainfall, should lie unimproved, and be at the present time for sale at from $5 – $12 per acre. And the wonder is all the greater, when we find that a railroad passes through the whole length of this tract, with several branches, and that no part of it is more than twelve miles from the railroad, and much of it within from one to five miles of it, and that this railroad is now offering every facility to farmers, to transport their produce to market, and to bring from the city the needed fertilizers. The shores of the island abound in the best qualities of edible fish, oysters, clams, mussels, scollops, lobsters, crabs, etc., and the game birds and four-footed game of the whole region are abundant. On the island are forty factories for the production of oil from the menhaden, and the fish-scrap, or guano, one of the best fertilizers known, is now sent away from the island, because there is little or no demand for it there.

Why it has not been Settled Hitherto
The only causes which can be assigned for the non-settlement of these lands, are the apathy of the inhabitants, and their lack of enterprise, and the evil report which has been made, falsely, of the barrenness of the lands, by those who preferred to supply themselves with wood from these lands, rather than to have them cultivated and populous, and be obliged to purchase coal for fuel. This state of affairs is now passing away.

Its Advantages.
The land can be cleared at from $5 – $10 per acre, some of the timber being large enough for building purposes or for railroad ties. It will yield from twenty-five to thirty-five bushels of wheat or from twenty to twenty-eight bushels of rye to the acre, from two hundred and fifty to three hundred and fifty bushels of potatoes of the best quality, and with good cultivation and fair manuring, the whole region can be transformed into market gardens, fruit orchards, and strawberry, blackberry, and raspberry lands of the greatest productiveness, and for all these products there is an unfailing demand at the highest prices, in New York and Brooklyn and the cities adjacent.

Market-Garden Farming More Profitable at the East

With the same capital, a young farmer, who is intelligent and enterprising, can do better on these lands, than he can in Kansas, Minnesota, Dakota, or Montana, and can be so conveniently situated to the great city that he or his family can visit it as often as they please. The great summer resorts of Cony Island, Rockaway Beach, Long Beach, Fire Island, and Montauk, which are visited by nearly two millions of people every season, afford additional markets for produce. The island affords also great opportunities for successful manufacturing. The great city of Brooklyn at its western extremity, has more than $250,000,000 invested in manufacturing, and there is now rapid progress in the establishment of manufactories in the counties of Queens and Suffolk.

Not Adapted to Mining

There are not, at present, any known mineral deposits of great value on the island, whatever there may be in the future. The man whose heart is set on obtaining wealth from mining, will do better to go elsewhere; but even he need not go to the Rocky Mountains or the Pacific coast to find employment suited to his tastes, as we shall presently show.

New Jersey

If "Long Island's rock-bound shore" does not satisfy your longings for a new home, what have you to say to New Jersey? Just listen to a few facts in relation to the lands which can be furnished to immigrants in that State:

A Million Acres

There are more than a million of acres of uncleared lands in the eight southern counties of New Jersey, which can be purchased at from $5 – $20 per acre. They have been held by large proprietors, and most of them have their titles direct from the "Lords Proprietors," Penn, Fenwick, Byllinge, and others, who received their grants from Charles II. These great proprietors held their estates of from 17,000 to 80,000 acres of woodlands, and increased their fortunes by selling wood, timber and charcoal to the forges, iron furnaces, and glass-works of the vicinity. These great estates are now broken up, and the use of anthracite and other coals for the furnaces and glass-works, and for fuel, has rendered their former business less productive.

The Soil and Climate

The soil of these lands is good, a light loam, but easily cultivated; it can be readily fertilized by the use of marl, which is abundant in the immediate vicinity, and is worth from $1 to $1.75 per ton; lime, which is worth from twelve to fifteen cents a bushel; or fish guano, which is a very powerful manure, worth from $15 to $18 per ton. It will produce almost any crop which you may desire to cultivate, and yields fine crops of the cereals and Indian corn (thirty to sixty bushels of the latter), root crops, melons, market-garden vegetables of excellent quality, fruit of great excellence, and all the small fruits. Railroads traverse all these counties, and both New York and Philadelphia furnish excellent markets.

The climate is very mild, the mean annual range of the thermometer being only 431½° and the extremes being about 90° and 15° F.

Rainfall, Grape Culture, Manufactures, &c

The rainfall is about 48 inches. Ploughing can be done every month in the year. The culture of the grape is a favorite industry, and the grape attains great perfection from the long season without frost. The region is remarkably healthy and free from all malarious influences. It is especially commended for sufferers from pulmonary complaints.

Here are glass-works, silk factories, iron mines, artificial-stone works, iron furnaces, and a great variety of other manufacturing and mining industries.

West Virginia

If, however, you still prefer a country abounding in mineral wealth, turn your face westward or rather south-westward, and you will find in West Virginia, western North Carolina, or east Tennessee all that your heart can desire in the way of mineral Wealth. In West Virginia the most abundant minerals are petroleum, salt, coal, and iron, and all are found in the greatest abundance. The salt springs along the banks of the Great Kanawha yield a salt of the very best quality. The petroleum wells yield mostly the heavy lubricating oils, though some of them produce the lighter illuminating oils. The quantity seems to be inexhaustible. The coal is of several varieties, but all of excellent quality. The climate is salubrious and pleasant, except on the mountain summits, where the snow lies long. The mountain slopes are covered with valuable timber, furnishing the principal supply of black walnut and other hard woods to the manufacturers of furniture. The soil in the valleys is excellent, the rainfall sufficient, and the crops satisfactory. Land is cheap here, but the settler, though nearer the great markets than at the West, is very much isolated.

North Carolina

In her mountainous region, in the west of the State, has veins of gold and silver, which, though not very rich, yield a fair competence to the industrious miner. She has also mountains of mica, from which the best large sheets are procured; and some iron and lead. The soil is not very rich, and the method of tilling it is primitive. There is much timber in the mountains. The climate is agreeable, and there are valuable mineral springs at several points. Land is held at low prices, but its quality is not such as to make it very desirable.

East Tennessee

East Tennessee has valuable iron mines, copper mines, and coal-beds, and at several points is largely engaged in the production of iron of excellent quality. There is also gold, salt, and some petroleum in her hills. Much of her land is covered with heavy timber. Land is cheap, but the soil is poor, and requires fertilizers to enable the settler to procure good crops. But the mineral wealth of the region will eventually enrich it. Northern Georgia and Alabama have considerable quantities of gold and silver, but the ores are poor, or the precious metals have not been thoroughly extracted. These regions are not very attractive to the emigrant.

Florida

Florida offers many advantages to the settler in her fine climate, her generally fertile soil, and her early seasons. The cultivation of the orange has been greatly developed there, and is profitable to those who can wait for the maturity of the orange groves. This takes about ten years, and then the income is permanent and constantly increasing. Some parts of the peninsula are subject to malarial diseases.

THE MORAL

The moral of our long dissertation is, that with health, industry, enterprise, and economy a man can achieve a competence almost anywhere; without them, he will not succeed, even under the most favorable circumstances.

AMERICA AND GREAT BRITAIN

COMMERCE WITH GREAT BRITAIN – BRITISH AMERICA

COMMERCE WITH GREAT BRITAIN

The United Kingdom of Great Britain and Ireland, and its dependencies and Colonies, has always been our largest customer for our productions, and was for many years our largest creditor also, sending us her manufactured goods and receiving in return our raw materials, and thus having almost always a balance of trade against us, which we were obliged to pay in coin.

Of late years, the balance has been the other way, and a large portion of our bonded debt, held by foreigners, has been paid from this surplus.

It will be interesting and instructive to review this commerce for the 89 years of which we have record of it. In 1790, we imported from Great Britain, merchandise of the value of $13,563,044, and exported to her and her dependencies, merchandise valued at

$6,888,478, our exports thus being almost exactly one-half of our imports. Our total imports in 1790, were $23,000,000, and our total exports $20,205,156. Our total imports in 1878, were $466,872,846, and our total exports $722,811,815. Of this number, our imports of merchandise from the British Empire, were $157,244,953, and our exports of merchandise to the countries comprising that Empire, were $152,032,886.

In other words, our imports are about 12 times as large as they were in 1790, and our exports 65½ times as large. It will be interesting to notice some of the items which made up our early exports to Great Britain, and to compare them with the exports at the present time. In this way we can ascertain, in part, what have been our principal productions. The following table gives our principal articles of export to Great Britain, in 1790. Some of these were goods imported and re-exported by us:

Exports from the US to Great Britain during the Fiscal Year, ended Sept. 1790

	Quantity.	Value.
Tobacco, hogsheads......................	73,708	$2,754,493
Cotton, raw, bales..........................	1,403	$47,428
Ashes, pot and pearl, tons...........	7,679	$747,079
Flax-seed, cakes............................	36,917	$219,924
Wheat, bushels..............................	292,042	$355,361
Corn, bushels.................................	93,407	$56,205
Flour barrels..................................	104,880	$676,274
Meal, barrels..................................	1,401	$5,435
Rice, tierces....................................	36,930	$773,852
Beef and pork, Barrels.................	154	$898
Bread, barrels.................................	201	$610
Butter, firkins,..............................	384	$2,310
Honey, firkins...............................	151	$906
Tallow, pounds..............................	156,708	$17,211

Oil, whale, barrels	1,738	$21,048
Oil, sperm, barrels	3,840	$60,000
Tar, barrels	71,077	$105,510
Turpentine, barrels	27,800	$71,240
Pitch, barrels	7,000	$13,920
Seeds and roots	unk	$1,242
Staves and heading	unk	$177,968
Lumber		$35,204
Timber, scantlings, shingles, &c.		$27,402
Leather, pounds	8,650	$2,316
Snuff, pounds	4,100	$1,394
Wax, pounds	87,294	$21,852
Deer-skins		$25,642
Furs		$35,899
Ginseng, casks	529	$32,424
Pig-iron, tons	3,258	$78,676
Bar-iron, tons	40	$2,936
Indigo, pounds	532,542	$473,830
Logwood, tons	216	$3,019
Lignum vitae, tons	75	$750
Mahogany		$16,724
Wines, pipes	45	$4,425
Merchandise		$8,041
Unenumerated		$10,330
Total		$6,888,978

It will be observed that the great Southern staple, tobacco, soon to yield the supremacy to cotton, was of the value of $2,750,000, or 40 per cent of the whole export. Cotton, before the invention of the cotton gins, was but a very small item, its value being only $47,428 – nearly $34 per bale, though the bales at this time weighed only 150 pounds. The exports of cereals, wheat, corn, flour and meal, were a small amount as compared with our present export, but almost one sixth of the whole export to Great Britain at that time.

The amount of provisions exported is very trifling, in marked contrast with our present immense export. There was no marked increase in the export of cotton until 1796, when 5,628,176 pounds were sent to Great Britain. Seven years later, the export to that country was 27,760,574 pounds. The same year (1803), 50,274 hogsheads of tobacco, worth $4,524,660, were exported to England.

Thus, cotton and tobacco made more than five eighths of the whole export. From this time till 1860, each decade saw a steady increase of the cotton export. During the 12 years since 1866, our exports of cotton to the British Empire, have aggregated $1,445,064,000, an annual average of $120,442,000, against $3,445,037,000 of exports of all kinds of merchandise to that Empire.

It was not till 1847, that our exports to the United Kingdom, began to exceed our imports. Since that date there has been but six years out of 31, in which we imported more merchandise from Great Britain than we sent her; these years were 1850, 1852, 1853, 1854 and 1855, and 1864.

Let us now give a list of our principal exports to the British Empire in 1878, by way of comparison with those of 1790.

A comparison of these two lists will show that while the exports of most of the articles which then were staples have increased enormously, a few have dropped out entirely. We do not export now, pot and pearl ashes, flax-seed, rice, wax, (nor till the present year, honey) whale and sperm oils, and very small amounts of seeds and roots, ginseng, or indigo, logwood, lignum vitae, or mahogany. We do export some wines, but they are of our own manufacture.

Tobacco, cotton, bread stuffs, provisions, tallow, furs, and naval stores have been sent to England the past year, to the amount of nearly $310 million; while mineral oils, which were unknown in 1790; wood in manufactured forms, oil cake, living animals, leather and its manufactures, iron and steel and their manufactures, refined sugar and molasses, hops, agricultural implements, sewing

Principal Domestic Exports to the British Empire in 1878

	Values.
Agricultural Implements and Machines...................	$1,102,293
Living Animals of all kinds...........................	$4,396,453
Bread Stuffs...............	$146,304,119
Carriages, Carts and Railroad Cars............	$685,022
Clocks.........................	$591,425
Coal............................	$1,871,277
Cotton, raw................	$117,014,743
Cotton, manufactured............	$3,299,405
Drugs and Chemicals..................	$967,438
Fur and Fur Skins....	$2,014,594
Hemp and manufactures of........	$825,135
Hides and Skins........	$673,615
Hops...........................	$2,122,983
Iron and manufactures of Iron............................	$4,266,740
Steel and manufactures of Steel...........................	$681,761
Leather and manufactures of Leather......................	$6,164,904
Musical instruments	$557,562
Naval Stores..............	$1,125,856
Oil Cake.....................	$5,076,550
Oils, mineral..............	$10,001,528
Provisions..................	$82,374,578
Sewing Machines......	$611,509
Spirits of Turpentine	$1,776,216
Refined Sugar and Molasses....................	$3,360,879
Tallow.........................	$3,240,469
Tobacco, manufactured and unmanufactured.......	$12,317,788
Wearing apparel........	$270,863
Wood, Timber and manufactures of Wood...........................	$8,464,287
Total exports	**$152,032,886**

machines, musical instruments, clocks, carriages and railroad cars, manufactured cotton goods, coal and hemp, are among the new articles which figure most largely in our exports, even to Great Britain, after the great staples.

A considerable portion of these new exports are the result directly and indirectly, of our Centennial Exposition here, and that of Paris in 1878; and if we are careful to encourage our agriculture and our manufactures, and to make known our products to the world, it is not too much to hope that before the dawn of the twentieth century, we shall be the leading commercial nation of the world, and New York will be, what London has been for so many years, the financial Capital of the world.

BRITISH AMERICA

The territory claimed by Great Britain in North America, includes all that portion of the continent lying north of the northern boundary of the United States, except the territory of Alaska.

Its sub-divisions are:

The Island of Newfoundland

Newfoundland, though not a province of the Dominion of Canada, is partially in accord with it, and may be treated under the same general head. The Labrador and Hudson's Bay region are Territories, occupied at wide intervals, by trading posts or forts, and under the Government of the Dominion.

The Dominion of Canada

Consists of the Provinces of Ontario and Quebec – formerly Canada East and Canada West, or Upper and Lower Canada – Nova Scotia, New Brunswick, Manitoba, British Columbia, and Prince Edward Island. The North-western Territories are controlled by the Dominion, but not represented in its Parliament. These Provinces were united under one Government, by the Act of Imperial Parliament, passed in March, 1867, and which took effect July 1, of the same year. The seat of Government of the Dominion is at Ottawa.

The Executive Officers of the Dominion Government are a Governor-General and Privy Council of thirteen members, who also constitute the Cabinet of the Governor-General. The present Governor-General, who is the direct representative of the Queen, and answers to the Viceroy of India, though with somewhat more restricted powers, is *most Hon. John Douglas Campbell*, Marquis of Lorne, born in 1845, and married in 1871 to the Princess Louise Caroline Alberta, fourth daughter of Queen Victoria. The Marquis was appointed Governor-General July 28, 1878, and arrived in the Dominion with the Princess, on the 23rd of November, 1878.

His salary is £10,000 ($50,000) per annum, and a residence.

His civil establishment or personal Staff consists of:

Gov.-General's Secretary – Major J. De Winton, R. A.

Military Secretary, V. C. – Col. J. C. McNeill, C. B.

Controller – Hon. R. Moreton.

Aides de Camp – Capt. V. Cater, 91st Foot; Hon. C. Harbord, Scots Fusilier Guards.

Dominion Aides de Camp – Lt.-Col. Hewitt Bernard, C. M. G.; Capt. G. R. Layton.

Commander of the Forces – Gen. Sir P. L. McDougall, K. C. M. G.

Assistant Adjutant and Q. M.-General – Lt. -Col. A. S. Cameron, V. C.

Aides de Camp – Lieut. J. C. Barker, R. E.; Capt. Hon. N. F. Elliot.

Commanding the Militia – Lieut.-Gen. Sir E. Selby Smyth, K. C. M. G.

Deputy Governor – Hon. Sir W. B. Richards, Chief Justice of Canada.

The Queen's Privy Council

for the Dominion, are:

Premier and Minister of the Interior – Sir John A. Macdonald, K. C. B. D. C. L. (Oxon.), Q. C.

Finance Minister – Hon. H. L. Langevin, C. B.

Minister of Public Works – Hon. C. Tupper, C. B.

Minister of Agriculture and Statistics – Hon. John H. Pope.

President of Council – Hon. John O'Connor, Q. C.

Minister of Justice – Hon. J. McDonald, Q. C.

Postmaster-General – Hon. Samuel L. Tilley, C. B.

Minister of Militia – Hon. Louis R. Masson.

Secretary of State – Hon. J. C. Aikens.

Secretary of Marine and Fisheries – Hon. J. C. Pope.

Minister of Customs – Hon. Mackenzie Bowell.

Minister of Inland Revenue – Hon. L. F. G. Baby.

Receiver-General – Hon. Alexander Campbell, Q. C.

Without Portfolio – Hon. R. D. Wilmot.

***The members of the Council (except the Premier) receive salaries of £1,440 ($7,200) per annum. The Premier's salary is £1,643 ($8,215).

Chief Justice of the Supreme Court and Court of Exchequer for the Dominion – Hon. Sir William Buell Richards, Kn't.

Puisne Judges – Hons. W. J. Ritchie, S. H. Strong, T. Fournier, W. A. Henry, Henri E. Tachereau.

***The Chief Justice receives an annual salary of £1, 646 ($8,230), and the Puisne Judges £1,440 ($7,200) each.

The Dominion Senate, according to the Constitution, consists of 77 members, *viz*; 24 each for Ontario and Quebec, and 24 for the three Maritime Provinces; two for Manitoba and three for British Columbia. Provision is also made for the representation of Newfoundland when it shall come into the Dominion. The Northwest Territories have no representatives or delegates in the Parliament. The members of the Senate are nominated for life by summons of the Governor-General, under the Great Seal of Canada. Each Senator must be 30 years of age, a born or naturalized subject, and possessed of property, real or personal, of the value of $4,000, in the Province for which he is appointed. The Speaker of the Senate has a salary of $4,000 per annum. Each member of the Senate receives $10 a day for attendance on the sessions up to 100 days, but nothing beyond. They are also allowed 10 cents a mile for traveling expenses. There are at present but 72 Senators.

The House of Commons, or Representative House of the Canadian Parliament, is elected by the people for five years, at the rate of one representative for every 17,000 souls. On the basis of the Census of 1871, it consists of 206 members, viz: 88 for the Province of Ontario, 65 for Quebec, 21 for Nova Scotia, 16 for New Brunswick, 4 for Manitoba, 6 for British Columbia, and 6 for Prince Edward's Island. The constituencies vary in the different Provinces. In Ontario and Quebec, a vote is given to every male subject being the owner, or occupier, or tenant, or real property of the assessed value of $300, or of the yearly value of $30, if within cities and towns, or of the assessed value of $200, or the yearly value of $20, if not in towns. In New Brunswick a vote is given to every male subject of the age of 21 years, assessed in respect of real estate to the amount of $100, or of personal property, or personal and real, amounting together to $400, or $400 annual income. In Nova Scotia, the franchise is with all subjects, of the age of 21 years, assessed in respect of real estate to the value of $150, or in respect of personal estate, or real and personal together, to the value of $400. Voting in Quebec, Ontario, Nova Scotia, Manitoba, British Columbia, and Prince Edward's Island is open, but in New Brunswick, votes are taken by ballot. The Speaker of the House of Commons has a salary of $4,000 per annum, and each member $10 per day up to the end of 30 days, and for a session lasting longer than this period, the sum of $1,000 with, in every case, 10 cents per mile for traveling expenses. Eight dollars per day is deducted for every day's absence of a member during the session, unless the absence is caused by illness.

The Dominion Parliament answers to the Congress of the United States, and its legislation concerns solely the National or Dominion affairs. Each of the seven Provinces has its own Lieutenant-Governor and Executive Council. Ontario, Manitoba and British Columbia have only a House of Assembly in addition for legislative action; but

Quebec, New Brunswick, Nova Scotia and Prince Edward's Island have each a Legislative Council and Legislative Assembly.

The Executive Council and *Provincial Cabinet of Ontario* consists of six members, *viz:* An Attorney-General, Treasurer, Commissioner of Crown Lands, Commissioner of Public Works, Minister of Education, and Provincial Secretary. The House of Assembly has 82 members. Hon. D. A. Macdonald, of Toronto, is Lieutenant-Governor.

The Lieutenant-Governor of the *Province of Quebec* was, in January, 1879, Hon. Luc. Letellier de Just, but his removal has been requested; there is an Executive Council of 7 members, viz; Premier and Minister of Agriculture and Public Works, Commissioner of Crown Lands, Treasurer, Provincial Secretary and Registrar, Speaker of Legislative Council, Attorney-General, and Solicitor-General. The Legislative Council consists of 24 members, and the Legislative Assembly of 65 members. The Seat of Government is Quebec.

Hon. E. B. Chandler, Q. C., is Lieutenant-Governor of the *Province of New Brunswick.* The Executive Council consists of 9 members, a President, Attorney General, Provincial Secretary, Surveyor-General, Chief-Commissioner of Board of Works, and four members without other office. The Legislative Council consists of 17 members, and the House of Assembly of 41 members. The Seat of Government is Fredericton.

The Lieutenant-Governor of the *Province of Nova Scotia* is Hon. Adams George Archibald. There are 9 members of the Executive Council (besides 8 retired members who may participate in its deliberations), viz: Treasurer, Attorney-General, Provincial Secretary, Commissioner of Public Works and Mines, Commissioner of Crown Lands, and four members without other office. The Legislative Council consists of 19 members, and the House of Assembly of 38. The Seat of Government is Halifax.

The Lieutenant-Governor of *Prince Edward's Island* is Sir Robert Hodgson, Knight. The Executive Council consists of 9 members, namely: Attorney-General, Minister of Public Works, Provincial Secretary and Treasurer, and six members without office. The Legislative Council has 13 members, and the House of Assembly 30 members. The Seat of Government is Charlottetown.

The Lieutenant-Governor of the *Province of Manitoba*, is Hon. Joseph Edward Cauchon. The Executive Council has 5 members, Provincial Treasurer, who is also Premier, Provincial Secretary and Attorney-General, and Minister of Public Works. The Legislative Assembly has 24 members. The Seat of Government is Fort Garry.

The *Province of British Columbia* has Hon. Albert N. Richards, Q. C., for its Lieutenant-Governor. Its Executive Council consists of 5 members, viz: The Attorney-General and Provincial Secretary, the Minister of Finance and Agriculture, and the Chief Commissioner of Land and Works. The Legislative Assembly has 25 members. Victoria, Vancouver's Island, is the Seat of Government.

The *North-west Territories* are so far organized as to have a Lieutenant-Governor, Hon. David Laird, and an Executive Council of 5 members, which includes the two Stipendiary Magistrates, and the Commissioner of Police. The Seat of Government is at Battleford.

Judiciary of the Dominion

The Dominion has only two Courts. The Supreme Court, or High Court of Appeal, composed of a Chief Justice and five Puisne Judges. This Court has appellate, civil and criminal jurisdiction within and throughout the Dominion of Canada. It holds, annually, two sessions, in January and June, at Ottawa, at which place the Judges reside. The Exchequer Court, presided over by the same Judges, possesses concurrent original jurisdiction in the Dominion, in all cases in which it is sought to enforce any law relating to the revenue, and exclusive original jurisdiction in all cases in which demand is made, or relief sought, in respect of any matter which might, in England, be the subject of a suit or action in the Court of Exchequer, on its revenue side, against the Crown or an officer of the Crown. In each of the Provinces, there are Provincial Courts of Appeal, of Queen's Bench, of Common Pleas, Chancery, County and Division Courts, more or less numerous, according to the population and necessities of the Provinces.

Area and Population

The area of the seven Provinces of the Dominion, and of the outlying colony of Newfoundland, and their population, in 1871, were as follows:

PROVINCES.	area, english sq. miles.	population, 1871 to 1877.		
		males.	females.	total.
Ontario......................	106,935	828,590	792,261	1,620,851
Quebec......................	193,355	596,041	595,475	1,191,516
Nova Scotia.............	21,731	193,792	194,008	387,800
New Brunswick......	27,322	145,888	136,706	285,594
Manitoba and N. W. Territories...............	2,947,923	....	....	125,000
British Columbia....	225,500	....	....	50,000
Prince Edward's Island......................	2,173	47,121	46,900	94,021
Newfoundland........	40,200	75,547	70,989	161,389
Totals	3,555,149			3,916,171

The population of the Dominion has increased with considerable rapidity since 1871. About 358,000 immigrants had arrived in the Dominion, up to the close of 1876, of whom 210,000 are known to

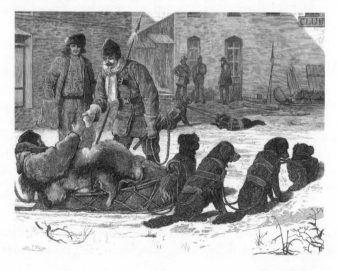

have actually settled in the Provinces–this is exclusive of the natural increase, as well as of persons who have migrated from the United States to Canada. The population of the Dominion and Newfoundland is now, 1879, probably about 4,500,000.

Imports and Exports. – In the year ending June 30, 1878, the total imports into Canada were £19,125,084 ($95,625,420); and the total exports were £16,298,267 ($81,491,335); showing an excess of imports of $14,134,085. The imports from Great Britain into the Dominion in 1877–78 were £7,584,480 ($37,722,400), and the total exports to Great Britain, £11,186,195 ($55,930,975). The trade with the United States was also very large, the commodities imported from the United States being of the value of $49,631,700; and the exports from the Dominion to the United States, $27,971,193.

Financial Affairs. – The finances of the Dominion of Canada have not been for some years past in a prosperous condition, though there are some indications of improvement. The public debt of the Dominion July 1, 1877, was £35,892,453 ($179,462,265); about $100,000,000 of this debt was payable in England. In proportion to her population this debt was as great as that of the United States, and in proportion to the wealth of the two countries, considerably larger. Since 1877, however, her means for paying it have largely increased also, and her relative financial position is better than it was two or four years ago. The extravagance and wastefulness of former Administrations is not likely to be repeated at present.

A railway has been projected, crossing the whole Dominion, from the Atlantic to the Pacific, intended to bind British Columbia to the Eastern Provinces, and the British Government has guaranteed a loan of $12,500,000 in aid of this enterprise.

Education. – The School systems of Ontario, Quebec and New Brunswick, are quite efficient and furnish primary instruction which compares very favorably with that of many of the States of the American Union. Nova Scotia, Prince Edward's Island and Newfoundland are less complete and effective, while those of British Columbia and Manitoba are as yet in an unorganized condition.

Higher education is very liberally provided for. There are seven universities, and fifteen Colleges, (some of them affiliated with the universities) in the Dominion, and a large number of  Collegiate Institutes, Female Colleges, Young Ladies' Seminaries, &c., &c. Most of the Universities have faculties of Theology, Law and Medicine, and several of them Scientific Schools also, presided over by eminent scientists. There are two Normal Schools and a model Training School in the Province of Ontario, and three Normal Schools in the Province of Quebec. There are also similar schools in New Brunswick and Nova Scotia. There are County High Schools in Ontario, and to some extent in Quebec and New Brunswick. At the close of the year 1875, there were in the Province of Ontario, 5,258 educational institutions of all kinds, with 494,065 pupils, and $4,212,360 was expended annually in their support. Of these, 4,834 were public schools, with 474,241 pupils.

Postal Facilities and Post-Offices. – There were in 1876, in the Dominion, 4,893 post-offices. The uniform rate of postage, of three cents, has been established all over the Dominion. The number of letters and postal cards sent through the post-office during the year 1875, was 34,510,000; the number of newspapers, 23,500,000. There are in all the principal cities and towns of Ontario and Quebec, Post-Office Savings Banks, in which any person may leave a deposit account, and may deposit any sum yearly, from $1 to $300.

Religious Denominations. – The Roman Catholics are the most numerous religious denomination, its adherents numbering, in 1871, 1,492,029; eighty-five per cent of these were, however, in the Province of Quebec, and they had a plurality also in New Brunswick. In Ontario the Presbyterians were most numerous, while the Methodists and the Anglican Church were not far behind. The Baptists are next in numbers to these three denominations, and there are also some Lutherans, Congregationalists, and a small number of several minor denominations.